Valentino Salvo

GOD IS GREATER
THAN YOUR HEART

THE FEAST OF RECONCILIATION

VERITAS

Published 1998 by
Veritas Publications
7/8 Lower Abbey Street
Dublin 1

Italian language edition first published 1991 by
Edizioni Elle Di Ci
Turin
Italy

ISBN 1 85390 324 8

Cover design by Lucia Happel
Printed in the Republic of Ireland by Betaprint Ltd, Dublin

CONTENTS

This will be the proof
that we belong to the truth,
and it will convince us in his presence,
even if our hearts condemn us, that
God is greater than our hearts.

1 Jn 3: 20

PREFACE

COME TO THE FEAST

'My sins are too great, Father. God cannot forgive them.' In this way the woman challenges me, with a great sigh which is born out of a heavy heart, burdened with human limitations. I talked to her about God's mercy, quoting the Old and New Testaments in order to make her realise that God is not so much interested in our sins, as he is in our will to accept his mercy and his love.

'But you don't know who I am; I have been a prostitute for more than twenty-five years.' I invite her to my home to rejoice and to drink a glass of good wine.

'But Father, am I not supposed to tell you what I have done?' I assure her that is enough and that we should celebrate.

Not only did this woman convert, she also became a nun. Now she works to rescue other prostitutes from the street. She tells each one of them, 'Go to a priest who will accept you with joy, who will not compel you to undergo a humiliating inventory of your sins. Just tell him that Ms ...... sent you – he will understand and he will celebrate with you.'

'Come to the feast.' I see the Sacrament of Reconciliation in this way: a joyful meeting with the Lord of life, who plunges us into his death in order to experience his resurrection. It is not a dry inventory of sins, but a song of praise to the immense bounty of the Saviour, who also uses our limitations to make us better people. It is not a terrifying meeting with a judge, but an encouraging relationship with a priest who is there to repeat the words of the apostle John: 'Though your heart accuses you of sin, God is greater than your heart'.

In order to celebrate the Sacrament of Reconciliation in a fruitful and joyful way, it is necessary to take a journey. You need to become a pilgrim, searching for that beauty and peace that only God can guarantee, showing us a journey in which a fall can be converted into an act of love. We decide to stand and look with hope at the sky above.

The journey towards welcoming God's mercy is well described in this book, written by a priest who was once my pupil. He became my friend and accepted my suggestion that he might work in Africa (which he did for fourteen years). I then called him to Rome, to the Alfonsiana Academy, in order to continue my work to spread the 'law of Christ', the law of love, and to find peace and joy, in being free and faithful in Christ. He is a priest who also travels the different roads of the earth like a pilgrim, to foster a culture of reconciliation and peace.

A pilgrim who welcomes the invitation to the feast is the vivid image which conveys the spirit of this book, written to invite Christians to experience the joy of frequent confession.

While celebrating this sacrament we still find those who are concerned to analyse how many times they have fallen, instead of asking how many times they have met the mercy of the Father who reveals himself in the people sent to us as angels and in unpredictable situations of daily life.

Why should we be concerned about our shadows, our limitations and sinfulness, instead of being joyful about our light, our grandeur and our goodness? After all, sin appears in all its gravity only when confronted with grace and love. It is only in the daylight that the pilgrim notices the obstacles in his way.

It is not only the penitent who is the pilgrim, but the confessor too. Both of them are called to an experience of love in the Sacrament of Reconciliation through the confession of sins and through listening to them while granting forgiveness. For this reason it is significant that the author starts and concludes his exposition with an autobiographical note, a public confession, which reminds us of the spirit in which St Augustine speaks about himself in his amazing work, the *Confessions*.

'A priest confesses his sin', says Salvoldi in his introduction, talking about his own crisis which found a solution in the desert – and immediately he knew that the pilgrim is not a solitary person who goes to the Sahara to find out where and how he made a mistake. Because his solitude is animated by the Word, by the teaching of the Church and by the spiritual presence of friends, he is sure that he will obtain the gift of God's pardon through their prayers.

In the spiritual pilgrimage towards reconciliation, a journey is proposed: 'from slave, to mercenary, to son'(St Gregory Nazianzen). This is a journey from the fear of punishment to the preoccupation of earning, to the intimacy of a son. These would be difficult passages if there were not a father to run towards the prodigal son, if there were not a Son to carry us on his shoulders, if there were not a Spirit of Love gently whispering words of consolation – words which encourage us to be reconciled with God, to let us be loved.

Nobody can merit love. Love is accepted with trust and through love we allow ourselves to be healed in order to pass from a sense of guilt (which is only a pure psychological fact) to a sense of sin (which is an act of faith, acknowledging that 'against you, you alone, have I sinned'). So, through the Sacrament of Reconciliation the penitent tries to recuperate the soul of bounty and love which is also hidden in his sin. His dialogue with the confessor is useful not only as a means of regaining hope and praising the Lord; it is also meant to allow a priest to help the penitent to recognise the goodness hidden in a situation which might, objectively, be considered pure limitation, pure sin.

It was a very great intuition of Pope John XXIII that 'every man is better than what he claims to be, is better than what he does'. For this reason we should avoid seeing only the negative aspects of ourselves or others or of the world. Goodness is much better than badness and the author suggests that we start each confession praising God for a particular grace, for a positive experience, for a specific gift received after our last confession. In this way the sacrament reveals the etymological meaning of confession as a trustful act of surrendering to God, who should be praised for his infinite mercy and for his great heart, ready to console us even when our own heart accuses us of sin.

Bernard Häring CSsR

INTRODUCTION

EVEN THE DARKNESS
IS AS LIGHT ITSELF FOR YOU
(Is 58:102 ; Cf. Jb 11:17)

Here I am, a priest in the spirit of St Augustine, trying to look at my life positively in a bid to clear the darkness within me and give praise and thanksgiving to the Creator, even from the experience of weakness and insecurity.

I was a young priest in Ibada in Nigeria teaching philosophy and moral theology in a large seminary of more than two hundred students. Seventy of them chose me as their 'spiritual friend'. I also took on the job of teaching biblical Greek and writing commentaries on the Gospel of St John. This meant that I had to work well into the night to keep abreast of my responsibilities. I was determined to fulfil all my duties in the best possible way. I didn't think of myself as a great sinner – no saint either, maybe I didn't 'sin' a lot, simply because I hadn't the time. (Perhaps, too, I was aware that if I got into sinful ways, I wouldn't have the moral strength to carry out my duties adequately.) I was proud of my celibacy and of my chastity which allowed me freedom to serve my neighbour, but this pride was ambiguous and no help to humility.

Little by little my prayer time shrunk as my duties increased. I said to God, 'What more do you want? I've left my family and friends for you. My lifestyle is not luxurious and I work well and hard. I'm preparing young people for the priesthood. So, all I'm doing is prayer in itself.' Oh, yes, I celebrated Mass, but often my intention was to shine – to stand out – by delivering captivating sermons and highlighting the aesthetic beauty of the Mass. I read the Breviary in both English and French, not so much to praise our Lord, as to continue to practise these two languages which I had to use constantly with English- and French-speaking students.

And, because I took for granted my own relationship with God, it seemed that when I called to him, I took his name in vain.

God had become for me a mere master-key – there to solve my problems.

In the past I had talked about our relationship with God as gratuitous, and about the need to give him all our time unstintingly. I had even taught that sin was not primarily an action, but rather a gradual slipping away from God and a cooling of the relationship with the Father until, eventually, it becomes so meaningless that the relationship dies. Sin is the breaking off of relations with God, often accompanied by the breaking off of relations with those around us.

So it happened to me. Little by little God became insignificant. Every now and then I would throw myself into efforts at prayer, but God remained silent. There was no more spiritual light in my prayer. And, of course, having weakened contact with God, I began to lose it with those among whom I worked too. I began to find my students annoying; I was no longer fond of them as I had been at first. Bit by bit they ceased to be lovable in my eyes. I began to notice their limitations and defects and this was no longer an experience of growth, but an annoyance. I was no longer interested in them and, gradually, the temptation to get out and form my own family and lead my own life began to make itself felt.

My sin? Presumption, inconsistency – hidden behind a façade of zeal for the service of Christ incarnate in the earth's disinherited.

I remembered then the words of Deuteronomy, when God reminds his people of their forty years wandering in the desert, searching for purification: 'Remember the long road by which Yahweh, your God, led you for forty years in the desert, to humble you, to test you and know your inmost heart' (Dt 8:12).

Yes, I would go to the desert, the very place where I could learn to love again, just as when I was younger. At least I could give God the chance to love me, always supposing that he still wanted to use me for his work.

Blinding sun, sand and more sand; silence, at times relieved by a sudden murmur of wind. The wind gathered force and whirled into sand devils. The desert became a sea of rippling sand and then the wind, grown to a howl, reshaped the dunes gently but irrevocably.

11

I needed limitless space and left my tent, which was pitched on the edge of the Sahara near Agadesh, an old centre for the slave trade. I really felt the need for solitude so that I could once more get in touch with God – re-open my relationship with him. And yet, in this 'empty' desert, I was hungry for human companionship. I wandered around aimlessly, praying that I would meet someone – anyone.

Then, on the horizon I saw a dot appearing and then disappearing. My first thought was that this was just another mirage; I had been tricked by this before. But this time, my senses were not deceiving me, for trudging slowly towards me was a Tuareg (a desert-dweller) heading for Nigeria in search of work – probably as a night watchman. He hadn't much with him: some water in a skin container, a little teapot, a small brazier, a very light tent. He was swathed from head to foot, only his light-coloured eyes peered out from the slit in his turban. He didn't reply to my greeting. Perhaps I had broken into a quiet state of mind which he had laboured to achieve.

He sat down and lit his brazier to heat the water. Each movement had the dignity of a priest carrying out a mysterious ritual. He listened to me, occasionally turning a peace-filled gaze upon me. Before drinking the tea, he poured a drop of water into his hand and cleaned his eyes. He lifted the veil covering his face and dabbed his mouth and ears. Each part of his body was thus symbolically purified while he whispered a prayer in Arabic. I knew the Muslim rite and, desiring to be in harmony with the Tuareg, asked if I could pray with him. He gave me a few drops of water and I, too, purified myself. Then we both knelt down and prayed, making many prostrations, acknowledging Allah – God as Creator and Lord of our existence. We drank tea and then, at last, the man of the desert spoke, in a quaint mixture of Arabic, French and English: 'I have left my tent because my wife and children are dying of hunger. So, I'm going to the city – a place I don't live in; life is in the desert with my loved ones.

'I could tell by the way you shook my hand that you wanted to communicate something; but to be able to confide in a person, you have to spend many moons with him; you have to eat a lot of salt with him.

'If you have come to the desert in search of God, be silent. Walk, don't set up your tent. And when you meet a nomad, look into his eyes; you will meet him again.'

As he set off again across the dunes, I thought of Abraham and his three pilgrim visitors under the Oak of Mamre, and how he recognised Yahweh passing by his tent bringing a message of hope. 'You will have a son.' My own hope came to life: I will be a man of faith, provided I continually convert and live with a new heart, regenerated and shaped by the 'desert'. I will give first place to the Absolute, and rediscover my own greatness, my identity and real value, through praising him.

The desert had presented me with a life programme: SILENCE, to put myself in harmony with the most eloquent silent – the Word made flesh. THE TENT, to live detached from myself and to empty myself so that God and my neighbour – my indwellers – become my only treasure. THE GAZE, in order to enter into a loving communion with a joyous community built on mutual trust and forgiveness, and my firm resolve to love with a new and purer spirit.

The Sacrament of Reconciliation which I celebrated at the end of my purifying desert journey was nothing less than a song of praise to him who had brought me from the slavery of self-contemplation to the freedom of finding myself mirrored in the many people I meet (never by mere chance) on my journey through life. Now that I have made a 'public Confession' (a must before launching into a book about the Sacrament of Reconciliation), I would like to begin by explaining how important it is to let grace dispel the interior darkness, and how beneficial it is to discover your own greatness in the praise of God.

I have begun by outlining my own liberating experience of recognising and accepting myself just as I am in the Creator's eyes. I will proceed with some reflections which tie in my 'Confiteor' with some very common queries of today: Is it really necessary to go to confession? Why do you have to tell your sins to a priest? The form of the Rite of Confession has changed many times down through the ages; so why can't it be changed again to suit the needs (and psychology) of today? Is oral confession the only way to cancel sin? Doesn't the Eucharist take away sin?

Those burning and vital questions call for serious philosophical and theological study.

There is nothing more effective than a personal experience for convincing us of the need to find appropriate ways of approaching the Sacrament of Reconciliation, and celebrating it with the joy of those who know that with this sacrament we plunge ourselves into the life, death and resurrection of Christ. If the sacrament is a meeting between the penitent and the love of the Redeemer, it simply cannot be reduced to an arid monotonous telling of a list of sins.

Since the words 'I confess' mean, above all, 'I acknowledge, I abandon myself, I tender praise', I must ask myself if my confessions have been filled with joy and praise to the Saviour or, contrarily, oppressed by the fear of having left out some sin and thus be facing eternal damnation. Have my confessions been a rite imposed upon me, or a good way of discovering that piece of truth and good and love which is present even in sin?

This is the point which I wish to clarify in this book, a book which echoes the invitation of the father to the prodigal son, 'Bring the calf we have been fattening, and kill it; we are going to have a feast, a celebration, because this son of mine was dead and has come back to life; he was lost and is found' (Lk 15: 23). This father is the figure of God for whom 'even darkness is clearer than light'.

1

MY SIN IS ALWAYS BEFORE ME
(Ps 51:5)

And you will be filled with joy (Dt 16:15)
There is a sinful way of speaking about sin: seeing it (in itself) completely separated from divine mercy, relating in no way to the super-abundant grace which Christ offers us to make us part of his love and joy. St Paul, in his letter to the Romans, clearly states, 'Where sin abounds, grace is super-abundant' (Rm 5:20). And St John has the same point of view: 'Whatever accusations our conscience may raise against us, God is greater than our conscience' (1 Jn 3:20). God uses sin to bring about the triumph of his mercy, to lift us from the dust and to raise us to a higher dignity than we had before we experienced our own evil.

To speak of sin outside of the context of salvation and redemption is to give too much importance to the negative aspect of this reality. If we tend to see sin everywhere and in everything, we are insulting God who, when he created the world, proclaimed that 'everything is beautiful'; who, at the end of his work, having given life to the first couple, 'saw that, indeed, it was very good' (Gn 1:31).

There is more good than evil in this world, but it is just not given coverage in the mass media, which thrives on bad news. And, if the Church doesn't want to follow suit, it simply must begin to proclaim a more joyous and positive message, and stop offending Christ and his Father by insinuating – indirectly – that the latter didn't plan the world very well. Moreover, the Church, through the Sacrament of Reconciliation, has a duty to offer its children a positive way of looking at their lives, recognising the common vocation summed up in the Old Testament in one concise sentence: 'You will be filled with joy' (Dt 16:15).

The infrastructures of sin

And what can be said about the essence of sin? John Paul II, in his encyclical *Sollicitudo rei socialis,* speaks of the sin of egotism of which we are all guilty to a greater or lesser degree. He also states that the evil in humanity is so serious and complex that it has built up a structure which holds us enslaved: the sin of our society expressed in the extreme injustice of spending three million dollars every single minute in the arms race, while every single minute, forty people are allowed to die of hunger. During his visit to the countries of the Sahel in 1990 (while in Burkina Faso), the Pope launched an appeal to the developed world to send aid to these arid lands. His invitation on that occasion to reflect on our 'fratricidal indifference' should make us all tremble.

Without a doubt, sinful infrastructures do exist. And whoever does not work to break this network of death is helping to reinforce it. However, even this burning and dramatic issue should not throw us into despair.

The fact that, at last, some opinions are being voiced publicly and officially in places of influence is already a step in the right direction. Today, some prophetic voices speak out against injustices. There are those who refuse to take up arms and, rather than do military service, they give some years of voluntary service to alleviate the wounds of human suffering.

People have not lost their sense of sin despite some priests' assertions to the contrary, based on the diminishing number of confessions and the fact that sins against the sixth commandment are confessed less frequently. Many people are convinced that it is much worse to take up arms than to indulge sexual weaknesses. The sixth commandment is still in force but it, rightly, takes sixth place, after the command to love, honour and respect God and neighbour, to love parents and, above all, not to kill, 'Thou shalt not kill!', and that includes 'fratricidal indifference'.

This present generation has discovered the gravity of social sin, and is eager to find an effective way of being reconciled with the Father and establishing peace with the Father, among its fellow men and with its neighbours. This entails going forward hand-in-hand to obtain forgiveness, and refuting the temptation to live happily unto oneself. It entails the creation of more just structures so that the 'cursed of the earth' no longer fall victims of our privileges (cf. Paul VI, *Populorum progressio*).

The first step towards celebrating the Sacrament of Reconciliation joyfully and fruitfully is when we become aware of our own personal sin and do not try to blame someone or something else, as when Adam blamed Eve and she turned right around and shoved the blame on the serpent. Each one of us must sincerely and humbly say: 'Against you, against you alone have I sinned; I have done wrong in your sight… My sin is always before me', as King David declared.

17

David – sinner and saint

David, the man, the king, is a baffling character. He catches the imagination and is rooted in the collective memory of the Israelite people, who regarded him as a symbol of the Messiah.

David interprets everything – every event, every person – in the light of the Lord. He praises the Lord when he has victories over his enemies. When he is in difficulty, he doesn't rebel against his situation; he doesn't kill Saul when he has him at his mercy (cf. 1 S 24:5-8); he understands that the Almighty transforms each suffering into a blessing: 'Perhaps Yahweh will look on my misery and repay me with good for his curse today' (2 S 16:12).

This man who is so magnificent and important for Israel, and indeed for humanity itself, which has made his psalms and prayers its own, touches levels of extreme weakness, wretchedness and sin. At the same time he is a faithful friend (recall his wonderful relationship with Jonathan: 'I loved you so much', 'Your friendship with me is more wonderful than the love of a woman' (2 S 1:26); he forgives; he is generous; he is ready to admit a fault, ready to humble himself; he is attentive to the needs of his soldiers; he is solicitous in praising the Lord.

Within David lives the saint and the sinner. He admits his sin and, in doing so, makes it an opportunity to come to his senses, accuse himself, humble himself. He confesses to the prophet Nathan: 'I have sinned against the Lord'. And Nathan answers: 'Yahweh, for his part, forgives your sin; you are not to die. Because you admit your guilt, the Lord forgives you' (2 S 12:13). David is so grateful that he bursts into song:

> Have mercy on me, God, in your faithful love.
> In your great tenderness wipe
> away my offences (Ps 51)

As I raise my eyes to you, Lord, I am more and more engulfed by your pity, your mercy and your love.

PITY: You gaze on me tenderly as a son does his old, dying parents.

MERCY: Your heart is good towards me; you forget the past and the guilt, and you give me an anticipation of trust.

LOVE: You give me perfect love in feeling that our friendship is not at an end; you are happier to forgive than I am to sin.

I thank you, Lord, for taking the first step towards me, for taking away my wretchedness.

> Wash me clean of my guilt,
> purify me from my sins.

My sin has made me so filthy and has contaminated my soul, and so, Lord, cleanse me thoroughly. Purify my eyes, so that I can see you! Purify my ears so that I can begin again to listen to your Word. 'Purify my nose that I may once again recognise the perfume of paradise' (Muslim invocation). Purify my lips that they may sing your praise. Purify my heart so that it will no more harbour sin. Purify my whole body, so that it will contain you worthily like a holy vessel.

> I admit my guilt,
> my sin is always before me.

I am so profoundly aware of the seriousness of my sin that I can do nothing but throw myself on your mercy and profound compassion. I tried to hide my sin and felt as low as a worm. I know it can be healed only if I come into the light and bare my wound to the sun.

> Against you alone have I sinned,
> that which I have done is bad in your sight.

Dear God, between you and me there was a beautiful relationship. Everything I have achieved I owe to you. My sin casts a shadow over something 'religious' and 'sacred': I have fouled up my relationship with you and neglected my responsibilities; I have broken the harmony of the community; I have wounded people that you love.

You are just when you pass sentence on me,
blameless when you give judgment.

As I admit my sin I acknowledge you as just in your sentence against me. It is easy to see that you have the victory over evil and you judge not to condemn but to redeem. My sin does not leave you indifferent; you are the injured party. You weep the tears of the innocent one. You suffer because your love is betrayed.

You know I was born guilty,
a sinner from the moment of conception.
Yet, since you love sincerity of heart,
teach me the secrets of wisdom.

Yet, let me find a small excuse: woundedness and weakness are part of my human nature. But I don't want to excuse myself. In the depths of darkness your light shines; you uncover my deceit and teach me wisdom. You want me to relish once again the joy I had before I sinned.

Purify me with hyssop until I am clean,
wash me until I am whiter than snow.
Instil some joy and gladness into me,
Let the bones you have crushed rejoice again.

My sin has drained me of strength; my bones feel broken; I've lost my dignity. So I implore you, Lord: purify me so that I will be better than before. May I become pure as the snow! Then I will be joyful again and I will rejoice at your altar, and my humbled bones will regain rhythm and dance.

Hide your face from my sins,
wipe out all my guilt
God, create a clean heart in me,
put into me a new and constant spirit.

I ask you not only to disregard my sin but to forget it altogether. Do more, Lord; be my creator once again and restore my original purity, vigour and joy. I stand amazed, full of wonder, as I see your pardon and my re-creation: my sin exists no more.

Do not banish me from your presence,
do not deprive me of your holy spirit.
Be my saviour again, renew my joy,
keep my spirit steady and willing.

When you took your spirit away from King Saul, you gave it to me. But now, please, do not take your spirit away from me. Don't deprive me of the joy of living in your presence. I ask nothing but to serve you, Lord, to love you and sing your mercy forever.

Your spirit is the love that gives me the strength to return to you, to allow myself to be reborn and to find peace only in singing your praises.

I shall teach transgressors the way to you,
and to you the sinners will return.
Save me from death, God, my saviour
and my tongue will acclaim your righteousness.

I want my experience of sinning and being resurrected to be of use to other sinners. So I mean to make my promise a song of praise and gratitude: May my tongue readily proclaim your justice and all that you have done for me, so that other sinners will take courage and find peace in returning to you.

Lord, open my lips
and my mouth will speak out your praise.
Sacrifice gives you no pleasure.

Lord, I repeat, I want only to praise you. This is your will. If I bring a sacrifice to your altar, you turn away your gaze; but you are never deaf when I sing of your love.

> My sacrifice is this broken spirit,
> you will not scorn this crushed and broken heart.

I can offer you nothing that you do not already have. The earth is yours; the sky is yours, the seas, the mountains are yours. All beasts and cattle are yours. I'm sure you don't need an offering of a poor little animal from me. As for me, the only thing that is all mine is my sin. I offer it to you in humility, certain that you will not spurn me. You are the only one who understands me.

> Show your favour graciously to Zion,
> rebuild the walls of Jerusalem.
> Then there will be proper sacrifice to please you –
> a holocaust and whole oblation –
> and young bulls to be offered on your altar.

Now that we are finally reconciled, please hear my plea for the whole people and accept the sacrifices they present to you. Accept the community which has come together to feast and joyfully eat a meal, singing hymns to your mercy.

Happy the man

> Happy the man whose fault is forgiven,
> whose sin is blotted out;
> Happy the man whom Yahweh accuses of no guilt,
> whose spirit is incapable of deceit.

> All the time I kept silent,
> my bones were wasting away
> with groans day in, day out;
> day and night your hand lay heavy on me;
> my heart grew parched as stubble
> in summer drought.

At last I admitted to you I had sinned;
no longer concealing my guilt,
I said, I will go to Yahweh
and confess my fault,
And you, you have forgiven the wrong I did,
have pardoned my sin.

(cf. Ps 32:1-5)

2

THE SON OF MAN HAS COME TO SEEK OUT AND SAVE WHAT WAS LOST

(Lk 19:10)

The one who compares himself with Love discovers his own sin
John the Baptist did not know Christ in person (cf. Jn 1:31-33) yet, when their eyes met as the Messiah stood in line to be baptised with sinners at the Jordan, he had no hesitation in proclaiming: 'Behold the Lamb of God, who takes on himself the sin of the world' (Jn 1:29). Through a revelation of the Spirit, the gaze of Christ had communicated life and love.

God steeps us in his love; this love is a gift, given solely out of the need of Love itself to communicate. God's love does not wait to be loved before giving itself; God takes the first step. He does not choose the lovable; he chooses the wretched whose only chance of rediscovering hope is God himself. Love has no pre-conditions; it is creative ecstasy. It is itself the will to set free. It is the power, the strength, the virtue which raises from abjectness, glorifies and renders equal those it loves.

Christ ate with sinners; he let the prostitute wash his feet; he invited himself to Zacchaeus' house. He spoke to the Samaritan woman at the well, the one who gave no hint about the existence of five husbands... And to anyone who was scandalised at any of this, Christ replied with a paradox: 'Blessed is he who is not scandalised in me!... I have come to save the lost ones' (Lk 19:10) and, again: 'The healthy do not need a doctor; the sick do' (Lk 5: 31).

The Son of God loves with a redeeming love all those who open their hearts to receive his mercy and who admit their need of him, saying: 'Lord, I believe; increase my faith'. 'Lord, that I may hear.' 'Lord, that I may see!' 'Lord, if you want to, you can heal me.' Jesus comes bringing complete salvation; he forgives the sin and restores physical health to show that he has the power to heal both the unseen sin-damage and the all-too-evident physical illness.

He has no desire to humiliate any person in his sinfulness; he gives a sign so that the sinner can see the contrast between his own wretchedness and the Light. The person who has the courage to acknowledge the goodness, love and mercy of God will become aware of his own sinfulness.

At the moment of the miraculous catch of fish, Peter is profoundly and painfully aware of his own sinfulness. At the sight of the fish, 'Peter fell at the knees of Jesus saying, "Leave me, Lord, I am a sinful man"'. With Zacchaeus it is Christ who takes the initiative. As if he were the one who needed this sinner, he asked for Zacchaeus' hospitality. Zacchaeus intuitively senses the delicate love which asked for hospitality so that he would not be humiliated, and his heart was won: 'I will give half of my goods to the poor, and if I have cheated anybody I will pay him back four times the amount.'

The focus of the parable of the Prodigal Son is not the story of a son who runs away from home, sins and then returns repentant, but the drama of a father who waits and longs for his son's return.

He sees his son – still a good distance away – coming. His heart swells with emotion. He runs to meet the boy, throws his arms around his neck. He has him dressed in the finest clothes; he throws a big celebration. He is happy because he knows his son has returned to him, counting on his father's love. He knows that it is his own love which has made his son come back. Distance and the long waiting have increased the father's love for his son (cf. Lk 15:11-32).

As in the three episodes above, once again it is Luke who tells us of the love-bond between Jesus and the sinful woman (Lk 7:36-50). The central phrase 'Much has been forgiven her because she has shown such great love', reveals a great deal. She loves greatly, in fact, because she has discovered that she is loved by a person very different from everyone else she has ever met. Here is someone who loves her, not with that 'love' which deceives the senses for a short time, leaving a larger void than ever within, but with a free love, which desires and works for the total good of the other. Also, in this instance, when the woman sees herself reflected in the love of the Master, she becomes aware of her true state and is filled with the desire to give herself completely to this love which does not deceive.

John the Evangelist is on the same wavelength. He underlines the great sensitivity of Christ when he guides the Samaritan woman to understand her state in the light of the truth that liberates. The woman is led to discover her sinful situation not through an accusation – that would have wounded and humiliated her – but through a proposal: 'If you only knew God's gift!' (Jn 4:10).

At Jacob's well, Christ has no bucket and so cannot get water; he gives 'living water', he offers his love freely, giving wings to the Samaritan woman's feet: 'Come and see a man who has told me everything I ever did; I wonder if he is the Christ?' The sinner becomes a missionary!

And what is more beautiful and more apt than the relationship between Christ and Simon Peter to demonstrate that solicitous love induces conversion and puts a person on the road to sanctity? The head of the apostles is certainly very generous, and without doubt loves his master, but he is also impetuous; he's afraid; he tries to calculate the risks; he does not accept the logic of the cross... he betrays Christ three times, which means 'completely'. But the Risen Christ does not reprove him; he goes up to him and begs his love: 'Simon, son of John, do you love me? ...Do you love me? ...Do you love me more than the others do?' (Jn 21:15-19).

The holy Church and sinners

If we compare ourselves with Love himself, we discover our sin, and we will also feel the need to be honest in our dealings with the One who 'has made us pass from darkness to light' (Col 1:13) and who calls us 'to be holy as He is holy' (Lk 19:2). The Church is holy, the mother who continues to generate her children through transmitting to them the life of the Son of God. And each member of the Body of Christ must be holy.

And what of those who sin and continue to fall into sin? Well, the same Peter who Jesus called 'blessed' because of his profession of faith, only a few minutes later heard himself called 'Satan' (Mt 9:33), because of his advice not to go to Jerusalem, not to face death. In this first among the apostles can be seen two sides: Simon, the sinner and Peter, the saint.

The same things can be said of Paul: he himself confessed that, on the one hand, he had visions which threw him into ecstasy and, on the other, that he suffered from a painful sting in the flesh, an angel of Satan who beat and humiliated him. 'Instead of doing the good things I want to do, I carry out the sinful things I do not want' (Rm 7:19). In the agony of his inner struggle, Paul cries out: 'Who will rescue me from this body doomed to death?' He does not supply an answer but instead offers thanks to Christ as the only one who can save him: 'Thanks be to God through Jesus Christ, our Lord.'

The New Testament presents us with a series of apparently contradictory texts regarding the Church. On the one hand, the Church is 'Holy, without spot or wrinkle' (Ep 5:21); 'it is a city which comes down from heaven, adorned as a bride' (Apoc 21:2). On the other hand, it is described as a community which is limited, which needs continuous perfection, which is made up of lots of sinners who have to be dealt with firmly so that they will not contaminate the other members: 'Don't you know that just a pinch of leaven ferments the whole dough?' (1 Co 5:6). Paul asks the Corinthians to ban fornicators from the assembly.

Thousands of pages have been written on the theme of the sanctity of the Church and the sinfulness of its members; this theme has caused bitter disagreements and heresies. Vatican II put the problem clearly into focus: 'As Christ brought about redemption in poverty and persecution, so the Church is called to follow the same path. It was essential that he should in this way become completely like his brothers so that he could be a compassionate and trustworthy high priest of God's religion, able to atone for human sins' (*Lumen gentium* 8).

At this point, I would like to explain briefly the impressions I have gained through reading the writings of the Fathers of the Church, in order to underline the truth that 'however great the number of sins committed, grace was even greater' (Rm 5:20) and, so, what really counts is not so much the sin as the forgiveness of that sin: 'If your heart accuses you of sin, God is much greater than your heart' (Jn 3:20).

The Fathers of the Church were not afraid to point out the distortions and corruptions within the Christian community. St Cyprian (priest of Carthage in the third century, defender of the faith and martyr) speaks of it explicitly in his *De lapsis*. Origen (a third-century writer on the Church who is considered to be the most learned member of the early Church) mentions it in all his works and gives a clear and concise picture of it in the introduction to his comments on the Gospel of St John. Eusebius of Caesarea (ecclesiastic, historian and scholar of the fourth century) states in the eighth volume of his *Ecclesiastical History* that, unfortunately, even among the hierarchy, the Church is not very faithful.

Often, when speaking of the Church, the Fathers refer to Rahab and Mary Magdalen – both great sinners – and seem to intend them as images of the human community before its meeting with Christ, who ransoms it and makes it his spouse. However, regardless of these considerations, it would seem that many of the Fathers were not so much concerned with the fact that Christians are sinners, as that they can be forgiven and receive from Christ abundance of life. They do not hesitate to affirm that even sin, once forgiven, puts the penitent in a higher state of grace than he or she was in before falling into sin.

A beautiful picture of the Church can be found in the bride of the Song of Songs. She is beautiful, intelligent and madly in love with her bridegroom (although, I think it should be added, she was not without a few defects, such as making the poor spouse wait just a bit too long before opening the door!). The Church is holy because her life comes from the Spirit of God and Christians are holy because they live of the very life of the Church in Christ. They are sinful but should not be obsessed by sin. Once they admit to having sinned, their sin is already a thing of the past. What counts is the newness of life in Christ.

St Irenaeus (second-century bishop of Lyon) describes the life of a Christian as a journey towards divinity. St Cyprian states that, once baptism has been received, the Christian must never look back, but always live projected towards the future: 'Become what you are. Become God's child' (cf. *Lumen gentium* 40).

All this can be summed up in the marvellous doctrine laid out in *Theopoiesis* (itself summed up admirably in the line: 'God became man that man might become God'). By contemplating the greatness and beauty of the new life in Christ, it is easy to understand the following enthusiastic expression: 'O Christian, acknowledge your dignity!'*

If we are preoccupied with the sin itself, we reduce the value of what the Redeemer has done for us: he has saved us through his love. True, the Fathers also put forward the idea of 'ransom', but it is marginal; it is an allusion which should be neither over-emphasised nor forced.

Christ came into the world not only to take away our sins, but, principally, to make us like himself. His presence within us defeats sin and the roots of evil. Of course, his presence should not be treated lightly, but maintained and sustained by an effort to be faithful to the God who searches us out, offers his love, floods us with graces and, when we do wrong, pulls us back with cords of love, as can be seen in the lives of many saints.

St Augustine's Confession of Praise

'Love and do what you please: if you stay silent, stay silent for love; if you speak, speak for love; if you correct, correct for love; if you forgive, forgive for love. Nourish the roots of love in your heart: this root can develop only into love.'

The only person who could utter such words, is one who loves and is loved: Love and do as you please. (The Latin word used by St Augustine for love is *dilectio*, which means 'strive for the good of the other', and that is precisely the essence of love.)

Philosopher, theologian, mystic, poet, orator, writer and pastor, Augustine has many of the qualities which I ascribed to King David and, indeed, it would be interesting to carry out a comparative study of the two. To discover St Augustine, all you need to do is read some pages of his many books. To discover the

---

* The Orthodox Church, generally speaking, tends mostly to concentrate on our becoming God rather than the sinfulness of the Christian. The very way in which members of the Orthodox Church confess their sins differs from Catholic practice, which still tends to measure, to calculate, to describe all the sins. To acknowledge our sinfulness and confess it to God through a priest – as we shall see further on – is necessary and very helpful. But the excessive fear (which smacks of scruples), the preoccupation with exactness in confessing sins, could derive from a certain pagan mentality which accentuates the effort to get rid of the sin instead of the joy of receiving free forgiveness.

sinner, you would do well to hear what his mother, St Monica, had to say about him. St Augustine says that it was she who converted him 'through her tears and prayers'. How many prayers? Augustine remembers his mother going to the cemetery to light a candle on the most forgotten graves (perhaps she thought that the dead could intercede for her family more easily as they were never 'disturbed'). How many tears? Her son was impulsive; he didn't want to study Greek and, from adolescence, he gave himself 'savagely' to the whims and fashions of the day and to dark loves, to such an extent that 'his handsome looks were ruined' (*Confessions* II, 1, 1).

'What attracted me more than to love and be loved?' (*Confessions* II, 3). Poor Monica, trying to dissuade her young son from seducing married women! Augustine himself admitted that he despised his mother at that time (ivi. II, 3, 7).

When he was thirty years old, Augustine fell seriously ill. He refused the Sacrament of Baptism, although he was heavily in sin. His excuse for this was that 'it is not ourselves who sin but some strange quirk of nature in us' (*Confessions*, V, 10, 18).

But, despite his many sins, Augustine always searches for God and desires to be searched for by God. This searching will lead him one day to write: 'We would not search for you, O God, unless we had already found you'.

Augustine recounts all this in the *Confessions* which he wrote to sing the mercy of God, to praise God and to proclaim: 'You have made us for yourself, O God, and our hearts will be restless until they rest in you'. He wants to convey to us that 'God is more intimate to us than we are to ourselves' and that God is the only reality we are searching for, even when we are seduced by passing delights.

'But what do I love when I love my God? Not material beauty or beauty of a temporal order; not the brilliance of earthly light, so welcome to our eyes; not the sweet melody of harmony and song; not the fragrance of flowers, perfumes and spices; not manna or honey; not limbs such as the body delights to embrace. It is not these that I love when I love my God. And yet, when I love him, it is true that I love a light of a certain kind, a voice, a perfume, a food, an embrace; but they are of the kind that I love in my inner self, when my soul is bathed in light that is not bound by space; when it listens to sound that never dies away; when it breathes fragrance that is not borne away on the wind; when it tastes food that is never consumed by the eating; when it clings to an embrace from which it is not severed by fulfilment of desire. This is what I love when I love my God' (*Confessions* X, 6, 8).

For Augustine, to confess meant, principally, to praise God who created us in such a way that even negative experiences would lead us to conversion. The 'Confession of Praise' does not mean that sin is minimised or dismissed. The burden of sin is taken on in full, but there is no agonising over it. It is seen in the light of God, who, as Manzoni says, 'never disturbs the joy of his children unless he is preparing a more certain and greater joy' (*Promessi Sposi*, chapter VIII).

The *Confessions* is not simply an autobiography; it includes philosophical, theological and mystical reflections. And its style and spirit is highly poetic, pervaded as it is by a thirst and nostalgia for the 'ancient and always new beauty' (*Confessions* X, 27, 38).

Let us consider for a moment Augustine's comment on King David's most beautiful psalm, the Miserere.

'Have Mercy!'

The fall of such a strong man must make us take stock of our own weakness so that we will not desire things which God forbids.

David saw the woman from a distance, but his desire was very close. What he saw was far away; what lured him to perdition was in himself.

Sin is in you when you succumb to its seductions; it is your master when you permit it to seduce you. It must be dominated if you are to avoid being its slave. You are safe only if your heart is protected from concupiscence.

You could argue: 'I resist strongly'. Do you think you are stronger than David?

We have seen what we must avoid, so now let us hear how to imitate David, in the event that we sin. There are lots of people who would like to fall as he did, but who refuse to pick themselves up like him. His fall is not the example to be taken; we must imitate his resurrection after the fall. Try not to make mistakes here.

The fall of the great should not make the small rejoice, but make them afraid. That is the aim of the tale; that is why we are told it; that is why the Church reads and sings this psalm so often.

Those who have not yet fallen listen to it in order to avoid falling; those who have fallen, in order to find the courage to get up again.

This great man's sin is revealed by the Church, not hidden. Those who understand it as an excuse for their own sins, have not understood its lesson. They say: 'David did it; why can't I?' So, using the example as a cover, these people act worse than David himself.

Let me explain more clearly. David doesn't use the example as a pretext; he succumbs to his passions without finding excuses. But you imitate David's fall, not his holiness. You love in David something which David detests in himself. You use the Word of God to do things which displease him. That is not what David did. The word of the prophet made him rise up again, not fall. Lord, you who receive incense in your abode, have mercy on me, in your great mercy, for your Name's sake, continue your work in me and complete it. Amen.

Late have I loved thee...

I have learnt to love you late, Beauty at once so ancient and so new! I have learnt to love you late! You were within me, and I was in the world outside myself. I searched for you outside myself and, disfigured as I was, I fell upon the lovely things of your creation. You were with me, but I was not with you. The beautiful things of this world kept me far from you and yet, if they had not been in you, they would have had no being at all. You called me; you cried aloud to me; you broke my barrier of deafness. You shone upon me; your radiance enveloped me; you put my blindness to flight. You shed your fragrance about me; I drew breath and now I gasp for your sweet odour. I tasted you, and now I hunger and thirst for you. You touched me, and I am inflamed with love of your peace.

3

FLOODED BY MERCY

Slave – Mercenary – Son

Neither saint nor sinner. That's how many Christians feel about themselves. But they forget that terrible indictment pronounced by God in the Book of the Apocalypse: 'Here is the message of the Amen, the faithful and true witness, the Prince of God's creation. I know your works: you are neither hot nor cold. But because you are tepid, and neither hot nor cold, I am about to vomit you from my mouth' (Apoc 3:14-16). Those who examine themselves in the light of the All Holy, and hear themselves called to be 'perfect as the Father in heaven is perfect' (Mt 5:48) and see the enormous difference between the Light and their own Darkness, between their vocation to sanctity and their own limitations, will very easily discover their own sin, which at best can be summed up in the words of the Lord to the bishop of Ephesus: 'You loved me more when you were young' (Apoc 2:4).

The Bible does not draw our attention to our sinfulness in order to humiliate us; nor does it wish to 'break our bones', nor even to instil fear in us. It simply desires to help us to understand and accept the absolute gratuitousness of God's pardon and to accept the joy which divine mercy brings, so that, having gained strength from the negative experience, we will increase our efforts to defeat evil through good.

To help us in our long journey towards holiness we are encouraged to turn to the wisdom of the Bible and the example of the Christian community which has held up for emulation the lives of many holy persons who testify to the mercy of God and point the way to perfection.

From the very first centuries of Christianity some of the Fathers of the Church, in an attempt to avoid discouraging sinners and to guide them patiently to discover what they have become through Baptism, describe three ways of serving God, which they borrowed from Plato.

St Basil (bishop of Caesaerea from 370 to 379) writes: 'I distinguish three different dispositions which inevitably lead us to obey. We keep away from evil because we are afraid of punishment; and so we are like slaves. Or perhaps we obey commandments because we are attracted by the rewards offered; so we are like mercenaries. And, finally, we may obey for the good (in) itself and for the love of the One who commands us to obey, happy just to have been found worthy to serve such a glorious and good God; and so we are like sons.'

To some catechumens who were a bit lukewarm and not very eager to ask to be baptised, St Gregory Nazianzen (bishop and doctor of the Church in the fourth century) said in a sermon in 380: 'I know three ways to find salvation: the slave's way, the mercenary's way and the son's way. The slave acts through fear of punishment; the mercenary thinks only of gain. But you must rise to the dignity of a son; you must love and respect your Father. Do good only for the beauty of free obedience to your Father, and don't forget that the reward is the joy of your Father' (Sermon 40, 3).

In the same century St Gregory of Nice (bishop of Nice) in his *Life of Moses* repeats the same concepts. And three centuries later St Massimo the Confessor (Byzantine theologian, mystic and martyr) also states: '…sons are those who, not for fear of threats, nor because they desire the promises, but because they are so inclined by habit and the soul's free disposition towards good (for love), they never allow themselves to be separated from God, just like that son to whom it was said, "My son, you are always with me, and all I have is yours"' (Lk 15:31), (Mystagogia 24).

And, finally, St Bernard (founder of many Cistercian monasteries in the twelfth century) sings and prays thus:

> Some men praise the Lord
> because the Lord is powerful;
> Some praise him
> because the Lord is good to them;
> Some praise him

simply because the Lord is good...
Lord, my God,
Let me rid myself of the heavy burden
of my own will.
And breathe
under the light load of charity.
Let me not be seized by servile fear
nor seduced by mercenary greed
But, guided by your Spirit,
the Spirit of Freedom, which fills your sons,
May my spirit enjoy the testimony of your Spirit
as I too am your son,
and your law is mine.

These saints bid the sinner not to be discouraged, but to use the sin experience to appreciate to the full the joy of returning to the Father's house, just as the prodigal son did. They echo the first letter of St John when he encourages the believer to abandon himself to love, without feeling crushed by sin: 'With love there is no fear, because fear presupposes punishment.... Anyone who is fearful is not yet perfect in love' (1 Jn 4:18).

St Paul also encourages the Christians to live the great honour and dignity of sons: 'The spirit you received is not the spirit of slaves bringing fear into your lives again; it is the spirit of sons, and it makes you cry out, "Abba, Father"' (Rm 8:15).

We often fall into the habit of acting like slaves and mercenaries. God bathes us in his mercy so that we can find the courage to break the chains which makes us bad. (The Italian word for bad is *cattivo,* from Latin *captivus,* which means a prisoner of war). That is, God's mercy frees us from slavery, from serving false gods and liars.

The journey towards the light
One day a man went into an Orthodox Church in Russia to admire the icons there. In the church there was a 'pope' giving a sermon on prayer. He quoted St Paul: 'We must pray at all times'. The visitor smiled to himself and went on admiring the icons.

However, the phrase he had heard simply would not leave his

mind; it became almost an obsession. He thought of that great apostle of the Gentiles, Paul, and decided to go back to the church and put some questions about prayer to the 'pope' he had heard preaching. However, his talk with this priest did not help him, so he went to consult the theologians (lucky man that he didn't lose his faith!). He even visited a monastery but, despite the long hours of reciting prayers, he was not convinced.

Then one day he met a *staretz* – a monk and spiritual guide – who was walking along barefoot and reciting a prayer. He, the seeker felt, was a man he could trust.

'What have I got to do to learn to pray?' 'That's easy', replied the *staretz*, 'all you have to do is to say three thousand times a day for a week: 'Lord, Jesus Christ, have mercy on me'.

At first the exercise was extremely boring but, little by little, this God-seeker became aware that the prayer was changing him internally and helping him to see others in a different light. At the end of the week he went to seek out the *staretz* and ask him the next step.

'You will continue saying the prayer for another week, this time reciting the prayer six thousand times a day. Let that be enough for you. It is very helpful to recite the prayer in the following way: while breathing in say: "Lord, Jesus Christ", as if to inhale God. Breathing out, say: "have mercy on me"'.

'So now', said the seeker, 'can I go on as I please?' 'No', replied the *staretz*, 'for a week limit yourself to saying the prayer nine thousand times a day.'

As he recited this prayer, the God-seeker's vision of reality changed; he saw people in a different way from before; he saw them just as God sees them. After twenty-one days of praying like this the man wanted to do nothing but pray. He dressed himself in sackcloth and went around barefoot. He worked to earn his bread which he washed down with water. On Sundays he treated himself to a little salt with the bread. And off he want wandering the roads of Russia, doing good, healing people and working signs of wonder, which are all told in the beautiful book written by an unknown author last century called *The Story of a Russian Pilgrim*.

This pilgrim found conversion in placing himself face-to-face with divine mercy. As a result he changed his lifestyle – he had been proud and independent but became aware of his sin and found his redemption in praying: 'Lord, Jesus Christ, have mercy on us'.

All the saints have one thing in common: a burning desire to boast of divine mercy once they have discovered their sinfulness. They are firmly on the road to holiness when they hold themselves to be sinners, unable to give love for love.

For a short time a person may force himself to be holy, and stumble about, and make a complete hash of it. The moment he becomes resigned to the idea that holiness is not for him and accepts his limitations is the very moment when he starts out on the road towards light, towards the very holiness he feels incapable of reaching alone.

The example offered by St Teresa of Avila is a good illustration. 'There is this child playing in a park. He trips; he falls and hurts himself. His father lifts him up, rubs his scraped knees, so that he can go on playing again. "What a good dad", I hear you say. But what about this one? A child plays without a care the whole day long. At bedtime as he undresses, he remembers having seen his father early that same morning, carefully putting away all the toys which could have harmed his son during his play. Which of these two children will be more grateful to the father – the one who fell and was picked up, or the one who had been spared the fall in the first place?"'

When I pose this question during a conference, I always get the same reply from most of the participants: it's better to fall and be picked up than live without the experience of pain. This is a clear sign that we are no saints. The saint is the person who knows he is in debt to God for showering her with his mercy and preventing the fall. She knows that without a love which forestalls misadventure, he would have been worse than the worst sinner. And it is to this mercy that he always runs, certain that without it he could fall at any minute. He knows that the nearer he is to God, the harder would be his fall.

That is why St Paul recommends: 'The man who thinks he is safe must be careful he does not fall' (1 Co 10:12).

I have sinned by omission

One of the most frequent sins – and the most serious, one into which we all fall to a greater or lesser degree – is the sin of omission: not doing the good that we could and should do.

God wants to make us the dispensers of his mercy, for our own advantage and for the benefit of all. And, meanwhile, we go on ignoring him – always thinking of ourselves. We live disintegrated lives, made up of a series of jobs and responsibilities which we rush into out of fear of being alone or of coming face-to-face with our own inadequacy.

We say in the Confiteor: 'I have sinned in my thoughts, in my words, in what I have done and in what I have failed to do'. It is painful to realise that many Christians do not even know what the word 'omission' means. Perhaps the blame is not entirely theirs; many priests sin by omission in not explaining the terms used in the liturgy, and don't tell people that an omission can also be a serious sin. The prophet may find it a very onerous duty to reprove the wicked, but he must not keep silent as it is his responsibility to be watchman over God's people.

'If I say to a wicked man: evil-doer you are to die, and you don't speak to warn the wicked person to renounce his ways, then he shall die for his sin, but I will hold you responsible for his death. If, however, you do warn someone wicked to renounce his ways and repent, and that person does not repent, then the culprit shall die for his guilt, but you yourself will have saved your life' (Ezk 33:8-9).

To keep silent, to do nothing to change the evils in the world today is to be guilty of serious omission. If, when we are faced with the sight (or knowledge) of a fellow human being dying of hunger, we shrug our shoulders and say: 'Am I my brother's keeper?', we are standing squarely in Cain's position.

Is there a person less gifted than ourselves intellectually, morally, materially? If we do not share these gifts with him, we are thieves. St Ambrose, a fourth-century bishop of Milan, stated: 'Anything superfluous that you have, consider it stolen from the poor'. The word 'superfluous' can refer to any kind of difference between us and others. In this sense everyone has something superfluous, since 'there is no one so poor as to have nothing to give, and no one so rich as to have nothing to ask for' (African proverb).

How many sins of omission are each one of us guilty of each day? This is no rhetorical question; I am only too aware of my own sin. Nor is the question intended to cause discomfort and doubt in the possibility of being able to free oneself from what Pope John Paul II calls 'sinful structures'. Underlying this whole line of reasoning there is one dominant idea: 'Grace abounds right where sin is greatest', or, to use a verse from the Old Testament: 'Come now, let us talk this over, says Yahweh. Though your sins are like scarlet, they shall be as white as snow; though they are crimson, they shall be like wool' (Is 1:18).

39

In another place Isaiah states that even if our sins were as high as a mountain God would make it a plain. And if our sins were as numerous as the sand of the seashore, God would forget them all because 'I have dispelled your acts of revolt like a cloud and your sins like a mist' (Is 44:22).

Yet, it is precisely this awareness of the superabundance of love and mercy of God which shows up to a greater extent the grievousness of our greatest sin of omission – our failure to run to a Father who is more eager to forgive than we are to be reconciled with him, a Father who has given us the Church as the protector and dispenser of his mercy in order to facilitate our attempts at reconciliation between ourselves and God, ourselves and the community, ourselves and the cosmos.

The Church – dispenser of mercy

The seminary of Bujumbura in Burundi stands in a beautiful park filled with a variety of plants and animals. One evening I was praying and walking in these luscious surroundings, reminiscent of Eden before the Fall, when I accidentally trod on a long, thick parade of ants scurrying about from one nest to another. It was a disaster; the little creatures started darting about all over the place, avoiding the area where their companions had met an untimely end. It was a general débâcle as the ants passed along the message of the disaster.

I was instantly reminded of the Indians who stroke the soles of their feet before entering a temple, asking pardon of the divinity for having, on their way to pray, inadvertently stepped on little insects. I longed to find a way of showing my grief at the damage I had caused, to help these little creatures out of their disarray. To do that, however, I would have had to become an ant....

This is merely a pale image of the mystery of the Incarnation: seeing the evil in the world (which, unlike the ant episode, God had no part in causing), God wanted to show his solidarity with us and rescue us from our self-made chaos: 'The Word was made flesh'. And when, mission accomplished, the Word returned to the Father, he wanted to leave behind him a way to salvation which would reflect our weakness – and so he left the Church, the petty, finite Church. This Church is for humankind a sacrament of Christ, precisely in the logic of the Incarnation – a concrete opportunity to meet the Absolute. The Church is the continuation of the eternal presence of the Word among humankind. This Word, who was born in a particular spot, in a precise time, continues in time in the Church – mother to all, teacher and dispenser of divine mercy.

All this obviously presents problems: the 'sacrament' is not completely identical to the sacred reality to which it refers. The Church, in fact, is very far from resembling the Saviour, although it will do so at the end of time when Christ returns to consign the world back to the Father, 'so that God will be all in all' (1 Co 15: 28).

Before talking about the Church as dispenser of mercy, it must be pointed out that the Church itself is the object of God's mercy; it constantly needs to be purified, as Vatican II clearly states (cf. *Lumen gentium* 8 and *Unitatis redintegratio* 6).

When it is said that Jesus gave the Church the mandate to dispense his mercy, the term 'Church' means the body of the faithful. However, the Fathers of the Church make it clear that the Son of God entrusted the ministry of reconciliation principally to bishops and priests. So the writings of the first Christians underline the duty of the hierarchy to carry out, in all humility and patience, this ministry of dispensing grace and pardon to all people.

The Holy Fathers are by no means lenient in their condemnation of bishops who are negligent of the all-round good

of their flock and do not guide them with mercy. They judge
harshly any bishop who uses his ministry as a privilege instead of
feeling the weight of this heavy responsibility. For the Fathers, the
bishop must be like God the Father, and also reflect the mercy of
the Saviour; he must reflect the compassionate face of Christ.

The mistakes of the first centuries have been perpetuated in
the subsequent history of the Church; but all her dark shadows, all
her lack of mercy and tolerance – from the Crusades to the
Inquisition to the weighty interventions of the Holy See – cannot
efface the splendour of so many examples of mercy dispensed by
so many Christians who were the humble ministers of
reconciliation.

St Augustine, with his first-hand experience of sin and the
overflowing mercy of God, always refers to the Church as a bride
'without wrinkle or blemish', but adds that she is not yet
completely holy. She becomes holy progressively, and will be
completely holy at the end of time. For the present she must
continuously pray 'forgive us our trespasses'. The waiting period
between now and Christ's return on the last day is the time of
mercy, and mercy is offered to all in abundance – and a touch of
fear too! 'Although the thought of my position in your regard fills
me with trepidation', says St Augustine to his flock, 'being with
you is also my consolation' (Sermon 340:1).

St Ambrose's secretary, Paolino of Milan, recounts that the
saint used to weep with penitents who confessed their sins to him,
because he felt that their sin was also his. He wept so much, in
fact, that the penitent was also reduced to tears. Yet, just as he was
wont to take on the sins of others, so he was also demanding the
making of amends; he forced, the Emperor Theodore to ask
pardon publicly for having ordered the death of the rebels of
Thessalonica in 390.

Now, leaping forward sixteen centuries, we can see the same
sensitivity in Padre Pio of Pietralcina. He was willing to spend his
life in the confessional; he did penance for those who confessed
their sins to him; but he was uncommonly hard on some
penitents, insulting them and ordering them out of the
confessional. And then he would go to confession himself and
pray that the penitent would return (and, indeed, the penitent

always did). Goodness, hardness, greatness and limitation, holiness and weakness.... This is Christ's Church, the one he has chosen to carry on his work of mercy down through the centuries. This is the Church which receives the grateful love of each Christian, even when he has to make his own the words of Erasmus of Rotterdam, the sixteenth-century monk, with that same faith, that same humility, that same emotion: 'I bear with the Church, certain that it will improve, and the Church for its part, is obliged to bear with me while awaiting my improvements'.

42

Bless the Lord, my Soul

Bless the Lord, my soul,
bless his holy name, all that is in me!
Yahweh, who does what is right,
is always on the side of the oppressed.

Yahweh is tender and compassionate,
slow to anger, most loving;
his indignation does not last forever,
his resentment exists a short time only;
he never treats us, never punishes us,
as our guilt and our sins deserve.

No less than the height of heaven over earth
is the greatness of his love for those who fear him;
he takes our sins farther away
than the east is from the west.

As tenderly as a father treats his children,
so Yahweh treats those who fear him;
he knows what we are made of,
he remembers we are dust.

(Ps 103)

4

CONVERSION AND SELF-ACCUSATION
(Ezk 18:31)

Convert and you will live
A dazzling light on the road to Damascus: Paul comes into violent contact with the Risen Lord.

A quiet conversation with his mother in the silence of the night, looking out to the sea at Ostia: Augustine goes into ecstasy and begins his search for the God of Jesus Christ.

It is a certain presence, burning like fire in the night: and God becomes a certainty for Pascal; he weeps for joy. He finds God.

It is a song during the midnight Mass at Christmas which catches the attention of an atheist walking by the church. Paul Claudel goes in and the question hits him like a thunderbolt: 'And if, after all, these people are right?' ...And he kneels down.

These are a few examples of the moment of conversion. Each one is unique and follows its own logic, but it is possible to discern a common element which can be subjected to the rigours of scientific study. I won't go into the investigations but simply outline a few common features. At the root of a conversion you can discover someone who is dissatisfied with his life. He reaches a crisis (often a crisis is providential as a period of re-ordering of thought, of taking stock, a painful cleansing of the being); the person starts searching for something new and then enters into a new bracing experience – an intuition – an enlightenment; something significant is read, a meeting with another who becomes a 'spiritual friend'; the person joins a faith community (without whose support the initial ardour would degenerate into delusion); he witnesses to his experience (encounter) with God, which changes his life.

The Bible is full of examples illustrating God's desire to call each person to share in his very life. God always makes the first move, as the human being is trapped in his limitation and cannot free himself without help. His situation reminds me of the Hebrew parable of the pelican whose big webbed feet are stuck in the mud. He tries to use his beak to pry himself loose; he frees his big feet but his beak gets stuck. He tries again with his feet – the beak is free but the legs are stuck once again. There is no way out.

All our individual attempts at spiritual take-off end in futility. We can make collective confession of our sin (cf. Jg 10:10); (1 S 7:6); we can do penance, accept punishment, to invoke the grade of conversion (cf. Jr 31:18); we may listen with joy to the words of the prophets who promise a new heart, a new spirit. ...All this gives us hope but it cannot actually free us from the mud of our sins. For this reason the Son of God becomes the 'pelican' in order to rescue the little trapped bird from the mud.

Why does God become human? 'To call sinners to conversion' (Lk 5:32). Christ begins his preaching by inviting creatures to conversion and belief that the Kingdom of Heaven has arrived with his coming (Mi 15:4); he joyfully places it on his shoulders, and brings it back to the fold – replaces it within the community, which, in turn, rejoices at the reunion.

'My God, have mercy on me, a sinner' (Lk 18:13)

When the chosen people realised that they had made a false move in their relationship with God and broken the covenant, they decided to make collective penance (cf. Jg 20:26; 1 K 20:31; Is 22:12, etc). They put on sackcloth, sprinkled ashes on their bodies; they fasted, acknowledging their unfaithfulness – an unfaithfulness as grave as adultery. The people had deserted the true God and prostituted themselves with idols; had abandoned the source of pure water, and suffered thirst at the cracked cisterns... (cf. Jr 3:13). The whole of the third chapter of Jeremiah (which the French ecumenical Bible entitles 'The Glorious Prostitute'), and from verse 19 on 'the Return of the Prodigal Son' deals with the unfaithfulness of the Chosen People, who admit their sin: 'Shame has devoured what our ancestors worked for ever since we were young, their flocks and herds, their sons and their daughters.

'Let us lie down in our shame,

44

let our confusion cover us,
for we have sinned against Yahweh our God,
we and our ancestors, from our youth until today
and have not listened to the voice of Yahweh our God.'
(Gn 3:24-25)

Later, John the Baptist cries out that all must acknowledge
their sinfulness and accept the sign of purification: baptism. This
must be accompanied by the good will to produce 'the appropriate
fruit'(Mt 3:8).

Before Christ worked a miracle, he wanted the beneficiary to
admit his need of help by proclaiming both his physical and moral
blindness, his inability to walk, his lack of faith, his guilt: 'My
God, have mercy on me, a sinner'. Christ insists that the person
acknowledge in words his sinful state, as the courage to expose
guilt publicly shows the genuineness of the will to be healed; it is,
in itself, a beginning of liberation. A person who talks of his
limitations feels better for it, even if he is not healed.

'Grace does not destroy nature.' On the contrary, it builds
upon it. The fact that the ancient synagogue, Christ and the
Church insist upon an external form of self-accusation points to
the human need to unburden self, even on the psychological level.
I will not attempt to demonstrate this last point, but I will
illustrate it with three examples – one from a film, one from a
series of experiences in many African tribes, and one from a
'confession' of a Muslim.

The film *God needs Men* is about the inhabitants of an island
who have no priest and so have to conduct their own religious
ceremonies. The sacristan does what he can to carry out the role of
priest and, one day, he is called urgently when a woman is having
difficulty giving birth. The good fellow puts the woman on his
boat to ferry her across to another island where at least some help
is available, but the woman is so ill that she fears she is going to
die. She asks the sacristan to hear her confession and he feels that
he cannot refuse as there just isn't a priest – he must take on the
role even in this case.

'I have sinned', confesses the woman, 'the baby isn't my
husband's.' The sacristan is quite surprised: 'Whose is it then?' he

asks. Just as the woman starts to blurt out the name, the sacristan interrupts her, saying 'a priest would not ask such a question…'. The woman was so anxious to get rid of the sin weighing on her for nine months that she was ready to tell all.

Many African tribes hold the belief that an adulteress who is having a baby must confess her sin to the midwife or the baby will be stillborn. Anyone who injures another member of the clan must make public confession in order to put things right with the spirits of the ancestors, the elders of the community and the offended party, who usually also has the right to claim any reparation he cares to. Usually he asks for an animal, small or large, according to the seriousness of the offence; maybe some clothes for his wife, and the food to feed the community who attended the reconciliation.

Sometimes when I supply for an absent missionary and am invited to a village to celebrate Mass, I witness scenes like the following: In the church, in front of the altar, while the people sing, the elders and the catechists discuss problems, especially concerning marriage. Although the people may not be able to hear the discussion, they all know every minute detail about everything concerning the couple in question. Sometimes a member of the congregation is called upon to testify. Quite often it has happened that, just as I was about to place the host on a communicant's tongue, the person has been violently hustled away by an elder or a catechist because he or she was not in a condition to receive Christ's body. There is a need to confess the sin, remove the obstacle, make up for the damage done to the whole community before the individual can be allowed to taste the joy of reconciliation.

An experience I had concerning a young Muslim lad is particularly significant here as it illustrates the need the human being feels to declare his sin. I will also give a brief outline of the discussion which followed the incident, as it throws light on some points which I will talk about further on.

One evening I was strolling along through a rich residential area of Abidjan. At the entrance of the residence of a minister of the Ivory Coast government there was a young uniformed guard who was studying aloud from a book on law while he stood sentry.

I said, 'Good evening', and he returned the greeting with a smile. He offered me his hand and when I took it he squeezed it and would not release it. When the required greetings were over, he proffered me a seat, saying that the night was long when you were alone and nothing ever happened.... He talked to me of his life and then began to ask me questions. He was studying at the university and had some knowledge of the Christian religion, which he admired, although he didn't understand the bit about celibate priests. However, he liked the idea of having 'men of God' who would listen. When he was a boy the priest in his village taught at school, and he, a Muslim, attended lessons on the Bible. One way or another, he took a liking to this Jesus.

As I made to go, he said that he wanted to share with me a burden weighing on his spirit – wanted to 'confess'. Since I am used to some form of syncretism in many Africans, and also since this unusual young lad had aroused my curiosity, I heard his 'confession'. Then I asked: 'so now, what can I do for a Muslim?' 'Nothing more, Father, I already feel good inside!'

I was amazed by this young man's capacity for interior awareness and the clarity with which he had related his inner situation, and I asked him what he considered 'good' and 'bad'. 'Good is everything which makes me grow; bad (evil) is everything which diminishes me.'

I asked him to list 'sins' in order of their seriousness. His reply mirrored what the Christians of the first centuries held to be so serious as to exclude the sinner from receiving Christ's Body: murder, adultery, apostasy (denial of the God of your faith).

Then it was the young Muslim's turn to ask me what I considered sinful: 'Breaking off relations with God (Allah), damaging relations with my neighbour, not loving Allah as Allah loves me and... (my glance slipped to the belt at his waist)... carrying a pistol, as you do!'

'But Father', he rebutted, 'Africa isn't like Europe; we have to defend ourselves'. So I explained non-violent defence to him, underlining the idea of the 'impurity' of carrying arms. 'Impurity?' he raised his eyebrows, 'The only impurity is not holding Allah in your heart'.

'And', I rejoined, 'how does a poor sinner reconcile himself with God and find peace once more in his heart?' The boy smiled and concluded: 'There are several ways to feel good inside: when you make a mistake, you tell Allah. If that doesn't put you right inside, you can tell someone, like I just told you. If I have offended a person, I have to ask his pardon straight. And since a sin offends the spirits of the ancestors too, it's a good idea to make a sacrifice for them in a solitary place, or on the bank of a river, or on a hill. In that way you make amends to nature too'.

From sinner to penitent

We have examined the steps a person takes towards sanctity. He starts by acknowledging his sin in the light of God's grace, which calls to conversion and gives a new heart. He then feels – even at the psychological level – the need to tell his sin to someone; the Bible insists on the explicit acknowledgement of having destroyed relations with God. Now let us consider what the Catholic Church has done over the centuries to dispense divine mercy in faithfulness to Christ's command: 'Receive the Holy Spirit. Those whose sins you shall forgive, they are forgiven….' (Jn 20:22-23).

There is no need to go into detail about the development of the Sacrament of Reconciliation; a general glance is enough to discern one constant element: quite apart from the changes in the form of imparting pardon, the Church has always demanded an external sign of contrition on the part of the penitent. Moreover, the most important element in the sacrament is not so much the analytical self-examination of conscience (this could be morbid and unhealthy) but rather the refocusing of attention on forgiveness and the magnificence of God's mercy.

Segregation – old forms of penance (first to fourth centuries)

The Church's practice can be summarised as follows: to be baptised meant to become Christ-like. How could you possibly break or drift away from him again? The Christian who committed grave sin was considered a sick member of the body of Christ who could contaminate the entire body of the Church. So he had to be segregated, put into quarantine. If he had gravely offended the community by renouncing the faith, or committing murder or adultery, he had to show his sinful condition publicly;

he had to do public penance in order to win pardon, which was usually extended only once in a lifetime: confession was considered to be a second baptism and so could not be administered more than once.

The Constantinian era saw the beginning of 'canonical penance'. The penitent was excluded from the Eucharist for a long period of time and had to undertake very severe penance: fasting, almsgiving, abstention from matrimonial relations for long periods (sometimes years), prayer.... When the period of public penance ended, the penitent was released from his obligations on Maundy Thursday through absolution imparted by the bishop, and was readmitted to the community during the paschal celebration.

Here it should be noted that it was the penance, and not the admission of sin, which was public. Sometimes not even the bishop knew what the sin was, although the whole community knew that the penitent had committed some serious sin which excluded him from the Eucharist.

This custom of the primitive Church shows the importance of the ecclesiastical dimension of the Sacrament of Reconciliation. However, the fact that the sacrament could not usually be repeated caused problems: people remained excluded from the Lord's Supper for long periods of time; people tended to confess on their deathbeds to avoid the harsh penance; inquisitive people tried to find out just what exactly was the nature of the grave sin committed: moreover, there was the risk of 'penitential and sacramental desert', that is to say, the Eucharist was received mostly by the newly baptised.

'Taxing' – penitential tariffs (sixth and eleventh centuries)

At this time the idea that it was necessary to confess only once in a lifetime fell into disuse. An example can be found in the practice of the Irish monks. In order to be of mutual help in the Way to Perfection and to gain the grace of the sacrament, the monks confessed frequently and in private to one another and they imposed 'fines' on themselves according to the seriousness of the sin.

These monks became missionaries in Europe and spread this

practice among the faithful. Most western bishops accepted this reform enthusiastically as, among other things, it was suitable to the uncultured barbaric customs of the time. The idea was that when a sin was committed, something had to be done immediately; the matter had to be sized up by a confessor. Each sin had a corresponding and precise expiation: a certain number of days or months of fasting. Of course, a person might commit a lot of sins and take up an 'expiation account' of several years before going to confession. This problem was tackled in several ways: ten years of fasting could be substituted by six months living in a cemetery. Another way was to pay some people to do the fasting. Or you could give an offering for the poor or the Church. It was advantageous to be able to go frequently to the sacrament of mercy. But the risks facing the penitent in this period were many and varied: too much importance was attached to external works; there was the danger of trading the ransom for sins committed: the abuse of the commutation of penance led to simony and made it easy for the rich who could afford to pay others to do penance on their behalf; there was an increase of individualism in the penitential process to the detriment of the spirit of community.

Caroline reform of the penitential system (late Middle Ages)
During this time the Church, seeking purification, set out to correct the deviation of penitential tariffs and re-establish a canonical practice. Public penance became the norm for the more serious public sins, while a type of tariffed penance, less severe than those formerly imposed, was required for secret (private) sins.

Extraordinary penances were imposed for extremely serious situations: to undertake a pilgrimage, on foot, to the tombs of the martyrs, or a whipping. During this period even 'confessions made to laymen' were used, although it must be said that the lay people confessed to were generally well known for outstanding sanctity. Perhaps it was more akin to spiritual direction rather than actual confession.

Private confession (thirteenth to twenty-first centuries)
In 1215 the Lateran Council imposed the obligation of a once-yearly confession on all Christians who had committed serious sin.

The doctrine, which is still practised in the Church, goes back to the Council of Trent (1551): the penitent passed from contrition to penance by confessing all his sins, which were pardoned through absolution.

Public penance was abolished and it was made easier to receive the Sacrament of Reconciliation, following the intuition of Rabano Mauro, the ninth-century archbishop of Magonza. He felt that the penitent's humiliation in reciting the sin was already a big penance in itself and so there was no reason for the further humiliation of public penance. Frequent confession aids spiritual progress, although it also diminishes the community dimension of sin and pardon.

Vatican II: from 'confession' to 'reconciliation'

After the Second World War the discovery of social sin (the absurd and barbarous devastation and the dropping of the atomic bomb) provoked a crisis in the traditional way of 'going to confession'.

Sessions with the psychologist or the psychiatrist are on the increase, while fewer and fewer people go to confession. Secularisation has played a part in deepening the concept of sin and the forgiveness which can be granted by a priest. In this context the Vatican Council addresses sin and conversion, updating, first of all, the language: rather than talking about 'confession', it prefers to speak of 'Sacrament of Reconciliation'. It speaks of sin in our life (*Gaudium et spes* 13, 37) and of penance at the service of the renewal of the Church (*Lumen gentium* 11; *Sacrosanctum Concilium* 109-110).

The Council prepares the ground for the renewal of the Sacrament of Reconciliation by inviting the faithful to turn to the Bible and become aware that sin and reconciliation should not be seen as isolated individual acts, since they have an undeniable community dimension.

The Synod of Bishops on the Sacrament of Reconciliation (1983)

a. The text that was discussed contains the following problems: the sacrament in question should be placed in the context of an alienated world in need of reconciliation. If sin equates with alienation, conversion is a means towards peace, unity and liberty in the sinner's life. The Church is the foremost place of reconciliation. Although the community plays an important role in accepting the repentant sinner back into the fold, the sinner must carry out his or her individual part by confessing to a priest.

b. The contribution of the International Theological Commission to the Synod rests on the following: conversion is a personal act, yet it has a social dimension. (By accepting from God the gift of conversion, the Christian purifies the Church and frees humanity.) Reconciliation takes place in the Church and with the Church. The study of the historical evolution of this sacrament leads to the conclusion that the various forms of penance correspond to the diverse situations in which the Church lives. Therefore, each historical period must emphasise the element which is most effective in helping Christians to reconcile themselves with the Father and with one another. Reconciliation with the community becomes a sign of reconciliation with God.

c. At the Synod the bishops gave pastoral rather than dogmatic guidelines: individual confession is important; it responds, among other things, to the psychological need actually to have contact with a person who imparts forgiveness. The self-accusation expresses the awareness of responsibility for personal sin, with no attempt to justify or to find a scapegoat. Precisely because it causes pain and shame and sacrifice, confession is a liberating act – the truth frees and heals.

d. The final declaration of the Synod states: the Church must become an efficacious sign of reconciliation and peace in a world which is full of injustice. In our reconciliation with the Church 'we celebrate and receive God's pardon and experience his healing love'. The sacrament frees us and allows us to serve our brothers.

e. One year after the Synod John Paul II wrote an apostolic exhortation as a kind of synthesis of the Synod, entitled *Reconciliation and Penance*. It goes back to the Council of Trent: the Sacrament of Reconciliation is the tribunal of mercy. The sacrament is a kind of judging action, although it has a therapeutic effect too. Confession of sin is necessary to obtain forgiveness. The advantages of individual confession are praised as this sacrament encourages spiritual progress, helps each penitent to discern his own vocation, and frees him from spiritual apathy.

The synodal process highlights some aims: to promote the Church's mission of reconciliation in all its aspects; to encourage the spirit of reconciliation; to encourage all peoples to work for peace and justice. By overcoming individual evil, humanity will make progress in all fields and the struggle for justice and peace will become a sign of reconciliation among human beings and, therefore, with the Father.

From this historical overview it is clear that the Church never abandons the sinner; it always tries to forgive him, adapting itself to his needs, changing the rite of reconciliation to conform to the needs of the time. It changes the form but the substance is constant: the desire to celebrate God's mercy, which uses a poor limited instrument – the Church – to guarantee in a visible way the invisible and mysterious gift of grace which creates a new heart and a new spirit where sin has caused destruction and death.

The knowledge and critical appreciation of the penitential action of the Church in the course of twenty centuries allow us to value the actual effort to encourage communitarian celebrations of the Sacrament of Reconciliation. In the future, if the signs of the times mature, there will probably be further changes in the form of the rite. However, one thing will remain firm – the principle that the penitent will have to make a gesture of self-accusation in a context in which the whole community feels itself involved in the process of conversion, and praising the divine mercy.

The Song of Moses

Think back on the days of old,
think over the years, down the ages.
Question your father, let him explain to you,
your elders, and let them tell you!
When the Most High gave the nations each their heritage,
when he partitioned out the human race,

he assigned the boundaries of nations
according to the number of the children of God,
but Yahweh's portion was his people,
Jacob was to be the measure of his inheritance.

In the desert he finds him,
in the howling expanses of the wastelands.
He protects him, rears him, guards him
as the pupil of his eye.
Like an eagle watching its nest,
hovering over its young,
he spreads out his wings to hold him,
he supports him on his pinions.

You have disowned the God who made you
and dishonoured the Rock, your salvation.

You forget the Rock who fathered you,
the God who made you, you no longer remember.

Heavens rejoice with him,
let all the children of God pay him homage
for God will purify his people's country.

(Synthesis of Deuteronomy 32)

5

BE RECONCILED
(2 Co 5:20)

Reconciliation: the 'kiss that burns'*
In Spain at the time of the Inquisition in the sixteenth century,
Christ turns up in the main square in Seville (where heretics were
often burnt at the stake), performing miracles for anyone who had
faith. The Cardinal Grand Inquisitor has him arrested and thrown
in prison with the heretics.

Night falls and the Grand Inquisitor goes to Christ's cell to see
him. He shoves the candle in Christ's face and asks: 'Why have
you come back?' He then follows this up with a long harangue, a
monologue, where he tries to demonstrate that the Son of God
has never really understood human beings – his mysterious being,
his limits, his need of 'signs'; that a human being is not pure
intelligence, and that, under the more or less mechanical impulses
of the brain there is a weeping, distraught heart; that man is not
free; he sells his freedom for a crumb of bread – sells his
conscience to get a small share of power, money, glory.

The Cardinal's accusations get stronger: 'Why did you not
give in to the temptation in the desert?' ...Man is so weak! It
might have been some help to him to know that even the Son of
God could succumb to a moment of weakness by accepting the
challenge to change the stones into bread, rather than present
himself to the world empty-handed, with the excuse that he didn't
want to deprive a person of his free will. The Cardinal reminds
Christ that there are no such beings as criminals – only hungry
people who need an idol to turn to.

Human beings look for a leader to whom they can kowtow –
someone who will regulate their consciences for them. Christ
could have had the whole world (third temptation – power) if,

---
* I summarise some ideas from 'The Grand Inquisition', taken from *The
Brothers Karamazov*, by Fyodor Dostoevsky.

even for an instant, he had bowed before the devil. But he refused power; he was ready to bow ONLY to the conscience of the individual. And so, 'blessed are the peacemakers' stands against power, which creates wars and conflicts.

All these beatitudes – comments the Cardinal – are just too much for us; we will never understand such perfect behaviour; we will never come anywhere near the ideal of being 'perfect as your Father in heaven is perfect'.

After this long harangue, the Cardinal expects a reply – an explanation. Christ is silent. The Cardinal threatens to have him burned with the heretics. The Son of God smiles and quietly comes close to the elderly Grand Inquisitor. He puts his hands on the red-clad shoulders. He kisses the Cardinal on the lips.

The Cardinal jumps back; his lips are trembling; he goes to the door, pulls it open and yells: 'Get out! Go, and don't come back… EVER!' Christ the Light melts into the darkness

And the Cardinal? 'That kiss is still burning on his lips.'

The kiss that burns is the sign of reconciliation. Here is a person in the throes of guilt, casting around for excuses and reasons, trying to be rid of limitations and badness and at the same time unwilling to break away from situations which, if not sinful, are at least ambiguous; and Christ intervenes with his disconcerting and disturbing mercy. That kiss is a sign of his love. But it burns; it is deeply disturbing; it makes it impossible to go on in the usual complacent routine and the offhand friendships which serve only to alleviate solitude.

God knows that a person is not pure intelligence; he knows that there is a great abyss between the things we understand and the will-power to act as we understand is right. So, he calls us and brings us back to union with himself, with our own selves and with all humankind by kissing us and offering us an experience of strong, disconcerting conversion. With that kiss planted on our lips, how can we remain wishy-washy and indifferent? No, we have to start changing and re-organising our lives; we have to begin to reshape ourselves according to the original project of love laid out for each one of us.

Reconciliation: putting the mosaic back together

The meaning of the word 'reconciliation', whether etymological or expressive of a symbol, lends itself to theological study. 'Reconcile' comes from the Latin: *re-cum-calare*, which means 'reunite, reassemble, put together again, recuperate' or, in other words, 'recall to stay with'. The picture which comes to mind is a broken mosaic with the pieces lying scattered around. On the wall a dim design is just discernible. The job is to put the little bits together again and make the original mosaic. When restored, the mosaic could turn out to be even more beautiful than it was before it was destroyed.

The tiles of the mosaic lying abandoned on the ground, covered in dust and trampled underfoot, are a symbol of a life which has completely lost its meaning. It is in such a miserable state that it cannot put itself together without aid. This miserable existence is like a great rock which, having broken off a high mountain, lies in a deep valley. It cannot return to its high place alone (cf. 'Christmas' by A. Manzoni).

A beautiful mosaic pleases the eye; dusty, broken tiles are depressing. A large rock shining in the sun on a mountain-top exudes a sense of security and strength; but a boulder lying on the valley floor is simply a discouraging obstacle. Only a great artist can restore a mosaic; only God Almighty can restore the boulder to the top of the mountain.

The story told in the Bible can be divided into three phases which repeat themselves with every new generation:

- God creates beautiful things;
- we destroys them and, in so doing, ruin ourselves, too;
- Christ, the Reconciler, restores the mosaic.

Christ raises us to our lost dignity – he makes us even greater than before, and more beautiful and more holy.

And what happens when sinners resist God's restoring efforts? The Lord begs them to let him love them and be united to him: 'God, in fact, in Christ was reconciling the world to himself, not holding men's faults against them, and he has entrusted to us the news that they are reconciled. So we are ambassadors for Christ; it is as though God were appealing through us, and the appeal that we make in Christ's name is: be reconciled to God' (2 Co 5:19-21). Here is the Father, seeking to reconcile us to himself, before we ask the Father to be reconciled. It is the proof that the destructive power of sin is so pervasive that it robs us even of the ability to extricate ourselves from it by ourselves. It takes an act comparable with creation itself: to forgive is a divine prerogative. Reconciliation is the crowning glory of mercy.

To be reconciled with God is to sing his praises

Often a wave of evil can engulf a whole family. At first they react energetically; they think that perhaps one of them has gone wrong.... With the second painful onslaught they can find comfort in the Book of Proverbs: 'for Yahweh reproves the man he loves, as a father checks a well-loved son'. But when death keeps on knocking at the same door and the family finds itself on a dung-heap, like Job, they have every reason to question God, as does the psalmist in Psalm 38: 'I am like the man who, hearing nothing, gives no sharp answer in return'. And if, in the agony of suffering, they happen to imprecate against heaven, he who holds the universe in his hand will understand 'desperate words which are swept away by the wind' (Jb 6:26).

There are people who have been stricken with sorrow so many times that, at a certain point they 'forgive' God for all that has happened to them; then, once they are reconciled with him, they commence to sing his praises. But, 'forgive God'? The expression seems quite blasphemous, but no one can really know just what a person tormented by suffering is really going through in the spirit. Nor is it always easy to distinguish the fine line between blasphemy and a desperate attempt to proclaim faith.

By this, I am by no means trying to excuse blasphemy; I am simply attempting to understand the mysterious workings of the human spirit which cannot easily be understood in the good-evil, virtue-vice dichotomy of Cartesian categories. Each individual has his or her own story, and each person is an enigma. When I hear confessions, I can feel two mysteries meeting: the penitent, the one who confesses his guilt – he is a mystery even to himself; and the mystery of God's love (at times I can discern even a third mystery – when my own 'self' emerges, rather than disappears, leaving room for mercy alone).

Anyone who turns to prayer after experiencing deeply perturbing suffering can be sure he is 'reconciled with God'. However, in the more usual way, 'reconciliation with God' means the tying once more of the bond of faith and love between the sinner and the Father after a personal experience of sin. At some point in our lives we enter a kind of 'desert' where we can barely distinguish between what is licit and what is not. Days succeed nights in a kind of hallucination, and then through the shadows and the light we discover that we have been ransomed from evil and mediocrity and we are on the way towards that day which will never end. The desert may still be a reality in our lives, but through the haze, tracks can be seen leading to an oasis.

It is at that moment, when we catch a glimpse of our goal on the horizon and hope gives strength to our footsteps, that we experience the joy of reconciliation with God.

On the Indian sub-continent – and probably in other parts of the world – many young people turn to religion after trying out various hallucinatory experiences, and there they discover the joy of reunion and reconciliation. They sit cross-legged in the lotus position for hours on end, in order to reach the depths of their own selves, deep down in the most hidden part of their being. They are submerged in deep ocean waves where all is perfect calm, while on the surface the waves howl and crash one on another.

Oh, to be reconciled with God, and find peace only in praising his name. Our life is made up of ever new desires and ambitions for more beautiful and more gratifying experiences. We soon get used to the experience and go hunting up further gratifications. Finally, we begin to tumble to the truth of God's words: 'Vanity of vanities' proclaims Qoholeth (1:2) – 'Vanity of vanities and all is vanity', except to love and serve the omnipotent God and sing of his mercy.

The experience of our ransomed finiteness, and the rising again from our miserable condition or, on the other hand, the realisation that we have not committed grave sins simply because we have been upheld by divine mercy, gives rise to the plea: 'Lord,

let me only praise you'. And thus is born the desire to recite over
and over again the psalms of the reconciled sinners:

> 'My mouth will sing your praise' (Ps 50:115)
> 'I mean to praise Yahweh all my life' (Ps 146:2)
> 'Praise Yahweh – it is good to sing in honour
> of our God – sweet is his praise' (Ps 147:1)
> 'Acclaim God all the earth,
> sing psalms to the glory of his name,
> glorify him with your praise' (Ps 65:2)

Be reconciled with yourself: stop doing yourself injury

Perhaps many of our woes and sufferings are self-inflicted simply
because we do not forgive and reconcile ourselves with our past,
our memories, our emotions, our bodies and our own death. We
haven't got enough faith and so when we commit a sin we torment
ourselves with the fear that God has not truly forgiven us. In this
way we show that we have a very limited idea of the Father. We see
God as some kind of policeman, complete with pistol in his belt,
keeping law and order and more ready to shoot than to come to
the rescue.

The basis of this unhealthy sense of sin may have started with
an unfortunate episode with a confessor who, instead of rejoicing
that a penitent has humbly confessed his sin, underlined the
seriousness of the sin and humiliated the penitent. This is very
unfortunate because, though the penitent has still a few steps to
take before he can 'contemplate the marvels of God's love' from
the instant that he asks forgiveness, he is already bathed in God's
mercy. When he says: 'Bless me, Father, for I have sinned', he
involves the priest in a mysterious event: the event of human
limitation coinciding with the Father's love. So, the confession of
sin should be greeted with a smile and rejoicing: this would help
the penitent to be reconciled with himself. It would give him the
strength to resist raking over the past, and that past should be
buried.

Reconciliation with self also acts as a healing balm to the
memory to prevent it from becoming a dung-heap, and fill it with
good things, like remembrance – Eucharist (thanksgiving). The

person who continues to call to mind the marvels of love which he has experienced at first hand himself becomes 'Eucharist' – a thanksgiving.

And to be reconciled with our own emotions. How many ups and downs there are in life! As children we receive affection, gratification and encouragement. A childish drawing done at nursery school is praised as a masterpiece: here is a budding Picasso! At primary school the usual assessments are, 'Very intelligent!', 'excellent'. At secondary school the 'perfect' pupils begin to lose esteem; and then, in the top classes they are considered 'dull'.

At this stage other factors begin to complicate matters: the spirit of the adolescent dreams of high ideals while the body has 'lower' aspirations and desires, stooping even to compromise and convenience and the pleasure of the moment. In this way the adolescent falls into a series of errors – all abundantly foreseen in the Bible: 'All the mistakes of my youth and ignorance, Oh Lord, forget them' (Ps 25:7). Certainly God does forget them. It is we who must reconcile ourselves with our emotions, especially as many errors are not exactly wilful and, again, ignorance diminishes personal responsibility.

To be reconciled with our own body means to accept it just as it is, with its merits and limitations. The French philosopher J. P. Sartre began to hate himself when, as an adolescent, he was forced to cut his long hair. He became aware of his 'horrible ugliness'….

Many people don't accept themselves as they are because their sole measure of beauty is the young people advertising toilet soap, perfume and beer on television. If they only understood that beauty is truth, goodness and self-control arising from the harmony between intelligence and emotions, then they would see themselves and others in a different light: they would discover their own unique beauty. In this reconciliation with their own body they discover a reason to praise the One who created all things good and beautiful: 'And God saw that I was very good'.

And finally, to be reconciled to our own death: when, on the death of a loved one, we decide to get used to the idea of death in order to love life itself, then, and only then, do we begin truly to live. Precisely because we have become aware of the precariousness of every relationship, as the Bible says, we are like the grass in the fields, 'fresh in the morning and withered in the evening'. We try to live to the full the present moment; now we love without putting off to an insecure tomorrow which, perhaps, will never come. We pray: 'Lord, grant me the grace to contemplate my own end, the limited number of my days: I want to experience my own fragility. I see how short my life is: Man is only a breath; he disappears like a shadow... so what can I expect, Lord? I trust only in you' (Ps 38).

Just as history is divided into years before Christ and years in the 'year of the Lord', so our individual history can be divided into 'periods before and after reconciliation with our death'.

All these levels of reconciliation take place each time a priest raises his hand to implore pardon: we are immersed in the life, death and resurrection of Christ; we allow ourselves to be reconciled with God, and our own past, and present. And then looking into the future, if we love life, we will have the strength to love even our own death, which is, after all, the hour of our true birth.

The liberating force of forgiveness

Quite apart from religious motives, the person who knows how to forgive and be reconciled with his fellows does himself a good turn – he heals a wound that would otherwise fester. St Paul said we should conquer evil with good (Rm 12:21). It is a wise and good person who repays an injury with a friendly gesture – an invitation to lunch, a box of chocolates, a bunch of flowers.... The gesture is so disconcerting that the 'enemy' can change into a 'neighbour', a defender, a supporter...even a friend. And so, instead of living in fear of another injury, the forgiving person has made another ally....

Some people are convinced that they have forgiven but that they cannot forget. Obviously, something will remain in the memory and involuntarily come to the surface on occasion. But, if the offended party does not make an effort to forget the offence this is probably because he has not completely forgiven, or at least, he is not fully reconciled, has not tried to piece together the mosaic in a supreme effort to create a masterpiece far superior to the original.

Many languages have a proverb that 'once a friendship is broken, it is difficult to put it back to its original state'. It is like a broken cord or like twice-boiled cabbages. But, according to the Bible, the very opposite was true between God and the chosen people, the Israelites, who had broken his alliance with them. The more a person makes mistakes, the more mercy God shows and the greater the feasting at the time of reconciliation. For God, to forgive is to forget and to cement a new relationship in a new spirit.

However, the argument for reconciliation with our neighbour must not be misconstrued as an invitation to be easygoing and complacent. It is true that 'mercy surpasses justice', but it is also true that if a relationship is to endure, it needs a full measure of truth and clarity and the re-establishment of order. Therefore, the obstacles have to be removed since nothing can be built on the quicksand of ambiguity. Moreover, it is important to find a suitable way to approach the offender and a suitable method. St Augustine said: 'You can forgive cruelly and punish mercifully'. Indeed, between true friends a great deal of strength of character is required not to forgive too lightly, but to be really severe in showing that the friend's actions are not approved of.

Human justice never forgives, it simply runs its course. Forgiveness and reconciliation shout aloud of the gratuitousness of love, and the 'folly of the cross', and the conviction that non-violence and love overcome all obstacles. Here, we have the logic of the Sermon on the Mount, the Beatitudes; here is Gandhi's *satyagraha* and *ahimsa* (power of truth and love): 'Your enemy will surrender, not when you run out of strength but when you refuse to fight'.

The aim of human justice is to re-establish order; forgiveness and reconciliation are based on a 'new heart' which will change society, and on the conviction that refusal to take revenge – to pay back an injury – is to include God in history by asking him to carry out justice. He is asked to intervene in human relationships as judge and lord of human destiny. In this way forgiveness becomes not only an act of faith, but a religious rite: the divine becomes part of human relations.

In this sense it can be said that forgiveness changes the course of history. Revenge provokes a vicious circle of violence. If there is no dialogue and no desire for reconciliation, wars are inevitable; blood will have blood. But, if we reject violent measures, we will win through and our love will invade our enemies and win them back even if, at first, it seems that they have succumbed. Martin Luther King used to say to his opponents that they could burn down the houses of their people, 'and we will love you'. They could carry off their women, 'and we will still love you'. They could smash in the heads of their children, 'And we will love you still'. He knew that love can redeem, ransom, overcome the aggressor without humiliating. In fact, the aggressor will be converted and reconciled to God and the rest of the human family through love alone.

Reconciliation among the Churches
At the foot of the Cross, when the Roman soldiers divided Christ's clothes among themselves, they did not split the robe. In this St John sees the symbol of the Church which must never be divided.

And when the Apostles, in obedience to Christ's suggestion, make a miraculous catch, they take in so many fish that their net nearly breaks. Here, again, St John, 'the disciple whom Jesus loved', sees an image of the Church which, despite all, will not break but will hold together very different types of 'fish' – the people of every race.

St John's dream was identical to the prayer said at the Last Supper: 'Father, may they all be one. Father, may they be one in us as you are in me and I am in you, so that the world may believe it was you that sent me'. But, it was not to be. The Christian Churches of Europe have been preaching Christ for centuries, while pulling his tunic to pieces and making his body one large wound. The divisions in the Churches have been exported around the world and are a great scandal to those who have even just a crumb of sensibility; they confuse those who have only recently begun to follow Christ; they encourage the syncretism of many African Christians who pass blithely from one sect to another: they do not understand all these 'theological fine points' which divide people in the name of Christ who died for the unity of the human race.

The ease with which Africans go from one Church to another has prompted some to think that, if there is a reconciliation among Churches, it will probably begin in Africa. In fact, I think that would be impossible since, as I have already stated above, reconciliation presupposes clarity in relationships, truth in the implementation of projects, and respect for the differences of individuals and communities.

At all levels, but most of all among the Churches, reconciliation is a gift which we must ask of God; it is the responsibility of all and not to be foisted onto any one group (we Catholics are fully aware that we have no monopoly on truth); it is the desire of all to uphold the autonomy of the historical responsibilities of each person, culture and religion.

The depth of understanding of the theme of reconciliation, whether by the individual or the community, can be gauged by the delicacy with which they approach ecumenism. We will be able to heal the wounds of division among Christians when we, as a community, humbly learn from the Gospel and admit that we – as a community – have rent the robe of Christ. And only when we have healed these divisions in reconciliation will we be able to stand up for humanity, to save the human race, to become peacemakers, to protect the environment.

Reconciliation with nature: praise of creation

This theme of reconciliation with creation is well treated in the final document entitled *Peace and Justice* of the Conference of European Churches and the Council of European Episcopal Conferences, written at the conclusion of the ecumenical meeting in Basle in 1989. Reconciliation can take place only when we admit – both individually and socially – that we have made mistakes.

'We confess our faults, as individuals, and as a society, when we follow Christ's teaching and become aware that we are entangled in a web of injustice, violence, waste and destruction. These are the fruits of human sin and they shape the future. We can cut loose from this web by confessing our common guilt. If, together, we turn to God, we will be given a new lease of life. The ecumenical efforts of the Churches towards justice and peace, and the protection of the environment, are based on admission of guilt and a desire to begin afresh.

'We have not witnessed to God's love for each and every one of his creatures; our lifestyles do not show that we are an integral part of God's creation. We have not overcome the divisions among the Churches; we have often abused the authority and power given to the Church by Christ to strengthen false 'togetherness', such as that manifested in racism, sexism and materialism.

'We have caused wars; we have not worked for reconciliation and mediation; we have accepted wars too easily – we have even dreamt up 'just causes' for them. We have not been consistent enough in investigating political and economic systems which abuse their power and wealth and exploit the earth's resources for their own selfish ends, thus forcing others into a situation of unrelenting poverty and marginalisation.

'Our sin is that we have thought of Europe as the centre of the world and of ourselves as superior to others. We have failed constantly to uphold the dignity of life and its sacred nature, respect for each individual and for human rights.'

When we have acknowledged the need to ask forgiveness for all these injustices which cause suffering to countless numbers of people and devastate nature, thus preventing us from echoing it by praising the Lord, we can begin to pinpoint suggestions and prospect for the future – for a more just world where everyone can live in peace.

Peace and Justice considers the problems concerning the protection of the environment and ways of living with creation. It states: 'Thousands of animal and plant species have become extinct. It is obvious that humanity has done irreparable damage to nature. In these last twenty years, scientific reports have tirelessly drawn attention to the harmful effects on ecology of the industry and agriculture of a technological society. Energy problems are immense. The rich North is faced with the need to change its systems of energy consumption. The greenhouse effect and the thinning of the ozone layer call for urgent and co-ordinated measures on a world-wide scale.

'We do not know how to handle certain doubtful scientific developments such as genetic engineering. Disasters and catastrophes such as Chernobyl and Bhopal, and the pollution of the Rhine have rudely awakened public opinion to ecological problems. Trees – whole forests – dying; streams and rivers and seas poisoned. These are the visible signs of the pollution which is carried across national frontiers by water and air. The consequent environmental problems cannot be resolved at the level of national governments. A new and international ecological order must be set up.'

'The Ecumenical Assembly at Basle, having asked forgiveness for sins of irresponsibility towards creation, points out that the re-establishment of harmony with Nature depends on our determination to: completely overturn the concept of continuous economic growth in favour of principles guiding the use of natural resources; force politicians and technicians to impose limits on energy waste; to discount nuclear power as the only essential energy source of the future, as it is socially, technically, ecologically and militarily risky; reconsider the Bruntland report which stated that it is possible reduce by 50 per cent per head the energy consumption of industrialised nations, and increase it by 30 per cent in the Developing World; draw up an international regulation capable of inspection, for eliminating wastes, especially nuclear; pass laws and implement rigorous controls on research in the field of genetic engineering; safeguard the diversity of species and the genetic wealth.

If we do not take this matter seriously, if we do not go through an 'ecological conversion', then all our speeches, all our words on reconciliation are in vain and even mystifying.

These very qualified proposals set out at Basle were highlighted at the World Assembly in Seoul in March 1990 in a much more tense atmosphere, in an effort to throw more light on areas of vital importance to the future of humanity. They could be usefully integrated by reading two more documents which deal with the same subject: the pastoral letter of the Bishops of Lombardy in Italy, 1988, *The Problem of the Environment*, and the encyclical *Sollicitudo rei socialis*. The latter gives a lot of attention to the theme of respect for nature and states that the individual's level of responsibility and moral sensibility can be measured by concern for ecological issues; it is the individual who must leave posterity a world where God's praise can still be sung in the words of the Song of Songs.

This sense of responsibility, of sensitivity, of praise of the Creator, are all found in the life of St Francis of Assisi. Around the age of twenty-five years, this son of Bernardone, whose pursuit till then was fame, glory and the pleasures of life, experienced a serious crisis at Spoleto where he witnessed the misery of many poor people. He was converted and turned to Lady Poverty. He followed the Gospel to the letter and chose to live a simple, poor life. In the presence of his father and his bishop he formally abandoned everything and, thus reconciled with God, gained the strength to be the instrument of reconciliation and peace with many of his fellow men, with the institutional Church, with Muslims, with nature herself. He spoke with Pope and sultan; he talked with children – with nature itself. He spoke to the wolf of Gubbio, which was tamed by the simple man; he spoke to a violent and brutal man; he embraced the poor and kissed lepers; he sang the glory of God manifested in the strength of fire and the gentle caresses of the wind and the purity of water, and tender even in sister death which ushers us into true life.

Many would probably agree with the French philosopher and historian, Renan, who stated: 'After Jesus, the Poor Man of Assisi had the clearest intuition of his filial relationship with the heavenly Father. His whole life was one continuous imbibing of divine love. His deep-set, clear, childlike eyes could see the ultimate secrets, those things which God has hidden from the prudent and revealed to little ones…'.*

Francis asked for nothing; he loved everything; his joys and his tears embraced everyone and everything. A little flower had the power to send him into ecstasy; nature for him was brother and sister. He beheld truth and beauty in all. We all know that beautiful song which he himself called 'The Canticle of all Creatures'. Surely it is, after the Gospel, the loveliest of poems.

Given the important fact that St Francis recalled humanity to eternal values and the inexhaustible wealth to be found in a heart which is reconciled with God, with itself, with nature, it is no wonder that the Basle document concludes with the prayer: 'Lord, make me a channel of your peace', and, adapting the text to the ecumenical meeting, ends: 'Lord, make us instruments of justice.

---

* O. Englebert, *La Fleur des Saints*, Paris: Albin Michel, 1980, pp. 324-25.

Make us channels of your peace. Make us the instruments of a renewal of your creation'.

There was a man

There was a man,
a clear-eyed man,
who gazed on all like a child.
He went barefoot
dressed in sackcloth,
and his smile was divine.

He walked, walked praying
along the banks of rivers.
He skipped over the stones singing,
His step was a dance.

He kissed the lepers,
embraced the earth.
He called the sun and the fire his brothers,
Water and death ... his sisters.
He sought comfort in the flowers
and voices in the silent stars.

6

MERCIFUL LOVE: ROOM FOR FORGIVENESS

The Sacrament of Reconciliation

In Victor Hugo's novel, *Les Misérables*, the bishop Myriel is robbed of his silver candlesticks. He meets the thief, who is chained between two gendarmes, and tells the latter to free the prisoner! 'He didn't steal the candlesticks; I gave them to him,' he declares.

Justice is treating people as they deserve for what they have done. It is also a restoring to right order, or re-ordering to God. Love, on the other hand, envelops them in such goodness that they are set free and recalled to life. Love is a challenge: it is the risk that Myriel takes, just as Christ does in the parable of the workers in the vineyard (Mt 20:1-16), where the later workers are paid the same as those who worked longer. Love does not calculate in human terms; it simply waits for the right circumstances to allow the water in the dam to overflow into the desert to make it flower forth.

Perhaps we need stronger and more beautiful metaphors to render even a faint idea of what takes place in the Sacrament of Reconciliation when a person whispers his sin and receives a joyous hymn to most merciful love in response.

The confessional is a place where the mystery of the death and resurrection of Christ is re-enacted and renewed. And this is the source of life for the penitent, who is not judged and condemned, but bathed in the gratuitous love of the Redeemer.

'Confession' should be a joyous encounter with hope; it should be sought after as a providential channel of personal and social peace. However, at the practical level, everywhere, on all continents, we are witnessing a continuing disaffection with this sacrament. After Vatican II the burning questions all over Europe were: 'Why go to confession? What's the use of confession? Who should we confess to? A man, just like us? We will just commit the same sin again. What is sin anyway?' These same questions are now spreading through Latin America, the Indian sub-continents and Africa.

Since the seventh century the system of private confession has been developing and the sacrament has gradually lost the ecclesial or community dimension. It has become impoverished and has lost the dignity of liturgical celebration. Certainly, after Vatican II community celebrations have refocused the attention of Catholics on the social dimension of sin and the need to approach the Sacrament of Reconciliation as a community; but there are still many areas to clarify and new roads to explore. Above all, the 'sense of sin' needs to be clarified. The concept of guilt, with all its psychological implications, should be scientifically investigated by psychologists and psychiatrists. But the concept of sin can be understood only in the light of faith. It is not only the breaking of a law or a behaviour which goes against moral standards, but an act against faith. Only within the mystery of God can sin be seen as a refusal to accept God's love: 'Against you, you alone, have I sinned' (Ps 50:6).

But how can God be affected by human actions? Since Christ identified himself intimately with humanity and since the commandment to love God is tightly bound up with love of neighbour, it follows that a breakdown in human relationships means a break in relations with the Father.

Each one of us is called to fulfil ourselves as persons by developing to the full all our potential, and responding joyfully 'to the call to become one unique reality in Christ and to bear fruits of love for the life of the world' (*Optatam totius* 16). If this does not happen, we taint our relationship with God simply because we do not allow him to be Lord of our existence; we do not allow him to make us holy and, therefore, instruments of the creation of a more just world and more loving community. A sense of sin can be felt only in the light of faith and love. We discover the true dimensions of sin when we focus on grace and forgiveness.

Another matter concerns the confessor's need to 'purify' the judgmental language he uses in the sacrament of Reconciliation. If the penitent feels judged and accused – whether implicitly or explicitly – the Sacrament merely increases an unjustified sense of guilt rather than a joyous meeting with God's mercy. If the relationship set up between confessor and penitent is judge-accused or master-slave, the meeting between confessor and penitent will be purely physical.

However, it must be admitted that this has been the case and still is, although in a milder form than in the past. Some strict priests believe that they help the penitent to gain a sense of sin by asking him sometimes embarrassing and disturbing questions. Happily, this is not very common; usually the confessor simply listens to and accepts the confession unquestioningly. Yet, on the other hand, complete silence on the part of the priest can also be negative. Some faithful say that they no longer go to confession because they get no benefit from it – not even a word of encouragement. A penitent is confused when the confession provokes from the confessor a negative sermon, which deepens the sense of guilt. He leaves the confessional with a feeling of dissatisfaction with his own life. He sees his sin as some monstrosity, with no relation whatsoever to the Lord's merciful designs. The same penitent may confess the same sins to another confessor and find himself confronted with complete silence. He begins to wonder if the confessor has actually heard the sin. He may repeat his confession, only to be told that the confessor is not deaf; he heard the sin the first time but didn't think it opportune to comment. If the accusatory sermon is negative, certainly silence is no more helpful as it makes the penitent think he hasn't been heard or, worse, hasn't been listened to. One way or another, despite the possible negative impact of some priests, the fact remains that the Bible depicts reconciliation as a path that leads not to judgment and a sense of guilt, but to a relationship with God through a meeting with the 'man of God' (the prophet – the priest) who should help the sinner to break away from his unruly life and allow himself to be guided by the love of the Father. The confessor is a bridge between divine mercy and human weakness; he is merely a channel of love. He is the mediator between God's invitation to be holy and our need for mercy. He is not in the confessional to judge; he is there to point the way to greater freedom. Part of that way is the humble admission of having erred, of having clouded the relationship with God, of having caused damage to the community of which the penitent now asks pardon.

Right from the Old Testament, God has been presented as the one who redeems, who ransoms and leads his people from slavery to the Promised Land. Not only does he sunder chains but he bequeaths to his people a 'land flowing with milk and honey'. So, in the New Testament, it would be completely absurd to talk of a reconciliation which includes a judgment-accusation phase. The New Testament announces a Father who sends his son into the world to take our sin on his own shoulders, freeing us from any sense of guilt and enabling us to celebrate with the community.

73

There is one final point to put into focus and that is the question of whether or not it is easy to commit a truly serious sin – a mortal sin. The saying goes: 'the just man sins seven times a day'. In the biblical sense 'seven' means 'many times'. Because our sins of omission are frequent, we may succumb to sin even 'seventy times seven' a day. If we live a lukewarm existence, neither hot nor cold, in an ambiguous and static situation, and yet are aware that our choices are gradually carrying us away from God, then probably this kind of life is steeped in sin. We can free ourselves from this spiritual death only if we allow grace to flow into us and make us change our ways.

However, if by 'possibility of frequent sin' we mean a situation which cuts us off radically from the love of God, before making such a judgment we must keep in mind a few points made both in the Bible and in the traditional teaching of the Church. 'Man judges by appearances; God sees the heart' (1 S 16:7). In his judgments, God keeps in mind our whole situation, our vocation, the things which condition us, our limitations and our intuitions. That is why he does not condemn but rehabilitates, and, up to the very last, pours on us his merciful love. According to human and ecclesiastical logic, the breaking of a law is a bad thing; it is a sin. In God's logic, the law has a value; after all, he gave it to us. But he has also given us 'the law of the Spirit' which extends beyond the law itself. He doesn't want us to be legalistic, in fact, referring to the obligation to keep the Sabbath holy, Christ added: 'the Sabbath is made for man'.

It is important here to highlight the basic direction of a

person's life: 'Blessed are the pure in heart' (Mt 5:8), meaning that God dwells in the pure person's heart. And as long as a person's heart is firmly attached to God, it is not easily torn away from him by an action which does not demand the mind, the conscience and the will.

Christ affirms, moreover, that evil comes from the heart, that is, from the intentions and a perverse will.

'The lamp of the body is the eye. It follows that if your eye is sound, your whole body will be filled with light. But if your eye is diseased your whole body will be all darkness. If, then, the light inside you is darkness, what darkness that will be! (cf. Lk 11:34).'

'No one can be the slave of two masters: he will either hate the first and love the second, or treat the first with respect and the second with scorn. You cannot be the slave both of God and money.'

'For from the heart comes evil intentions: murder, adultery, fornication, theft, perjury, slander. These are the things that make a man unclean. But to eat with unwashed hands does not make a man unclean' (cf. Mt 6:22-23; 15:19).

These ideas are developed in John 15, and in his first letter Matthew, too, points out that love is the sole criterion for judging whether or not a person is morally good or bad; love of one's neighbour is the basis of the Last Judgment (cf. Mt 25:31-46). The New Testament states time and again that the fullness of the law is love (cf. Rm 13:8; Ga 5:13-15; 1 Jn 4:7; 1 Co 13:1-13, etc.).

These are the grounds on which St Augustine exhorts the faithful never to eradicate love from their hearts: while the roots of love remain, it is almost impossible to commit such a grievous action as to cut adrift from Absolute Goodness. This is the logic which prompts Augustine to say 'Love – try to seek the good of the other – and then, do what you will!' Of course, he is talking of a love which goes well beyond the requirements of the law – to love as the Lord loves.

The same logic is expressed by St Thomas in his work *De Veritate* (27:1-9): 'While it is always possible for a person to lose grace, if his heart is turned towards God, it would be very difficult for him to pass from a state of grace to one of sin'.

We could go on adding examples and quotations, but it will

be enough to quote from the Penny Catechism: 'To commit a mortal sin there must be a serious matter, full knowledge, and deliberate consent'. All of these examples should reassure those with scruples who see sin everywhere, and convince Christians absolutely that we believe not in sin, but in the forgiveness of sin.

Bringing good from evil

'No one who is begotten by God sins' (1 Jn 3:9: cf. 5:18). St John considered it abnormal for a baptised person to renounce grace and commit serious sin. Abnormal, yes – but not impossible. But the Father trumps the reality of sin with the gift of reconciliation and caps all the advantages of this with another, not indifferent advantage: the possibility of deriving good even from evil. When a person begins to lose self-respect, to lose control of his own existence, to compromise, he very quickly finds himself in a web of misery and death. One compromise follows another and, bit by bit, he is ensnared. He sins. He is the only one who can judge the gravity of his moral responsibility. However, it might be opportune to ask himself if his action was all negative. What was the basic motivation? What was he looking for? What was the situation at the time?

By baring the soul to the Father, by letting the light illuminate the chaos of the inner darkness, by declaring the sin to a priest, one can, perhaps, not only accept the Father's forgiveness, but also regain the good hidden in the bad. If the sin consists of a gradual distancing of the person from love itself, the sinner, by offering himself to the Father, draws close once again to him; washed and purified, he can acquire some advantage.

Let's suppose that someone had fallen gravely into the sin of pride. A bad business; Almighty God is always ready to do miracles for the humble and 'pick him up out of his nothingness' and seat him among the high, but he's not the slightest bit soft with the proud. Christ praised the publican who stood bowed low at the back of the temple and beat his breast, but he had no time for the Pharisee who was puffed up with pride: 'He will go home with one sin more to his account' (cf. Lk 18:9-14). So, if a proud man goes on being proud even after confessing his sin, he will have to stop going to confession as there's no change. That's the way I am and always will be; my pride will live three days longer than I will – I do fancy a fine funeral! With a crowd of mourners!

But, even in this case, the Sacrament of Reconciliation can purify pride and benefit others. The proud man can say to God, 'I'm sorry; I've been proud; please pardon me. But what I did has been useful to someone. From now on, when I'm tempted to give in to my pride, I'll try to turn it into something useful for others. For example, if I want to shine as a good orator, I'll put a lot of effort into preparing my speech well so that those who hear me will gain something from my words.'

Perhaps the example doesn't fit every situation, but I think there is some logic in it: the sinner, with the help of the confessor, who should open up new avenues to God, sees his life in God's light.

Confession should not be confused with spiritual direction, but many, especially young people, will stop going to confession if they do not get help from their confessor in gradually overcoming their sins.

Good can be derived from a sinful situation, especially in the case of those people who do not habitually commit serious sin. But confession is just as valuable for them. Although the petty sinner remains near to God, he always has the feeling that he is not making all the effort he might towards perfection. So, for him also, the words of St John ring true: 'If we say we do not sin, we are lying to ourselves, and there is no truth in us' (Jn 1:8). The apostle is not necessarily alluding to grave sin; he includes the daily humdrum events, a mixture of large and small faults, high ideals and low results. If all this is regularly steeped in the death and resurrection of Christ through the Sacrament of Reconciliation, little by little our lives will come closer and closer to the Risen Christ and will draw nearer to the ideal of holiness to which Baptism calls us.

There is one other benefit to be had from humbly confessing our sins to a priest: it releases within us a sense of joy in and praise to divine mercy. It helps us to express our gratitude to the Father when, with the priest, we recite a psalm such as: 'Why are you cast down, my soul; why groan within me? Hope in God...' (Ps 42:5).

When we have finally arrived at the point where the Sacrament of Confession has become a sacrament of praise, we don't question any more whether or not it's worth the trouble to confess our sins, or to whom, or what to say. We take our cue from St Augustine and thank divine wisdom for having hidden from us the fine line between venial and mortal sin to preserve us from presumption. We enter God's presence asking him to accept us as we are and transform us into his image for the glory of his name.

77

Saints confess frequently, and the priest who is striving to become holy himself is always happy to be the minister of reconciliation. John Mary Vianney, tutored by the holy priest, Charles Bali, learned to read at the age of eighteen because he wanted to enter the seminary. After two years of effort there, the superiors sent him back home as he was unable to reach the minimum level required to become a priest. He was called up to fight in the war in Spain but, fortunately, he fell ill, returned home and took up his studies once again with the holy man who had presented him to the seminary before.

He was ordained a priest at twenty-nine years of age, more because of the dearth of priests at the time than on his merits. He was assigned to Ars, a little village of only two hundred inhabitants. He was not a very good preacher – his thoughts were expressed neither clearly nor attractively, but in the confessional he listened to people, he understood them; he inspired trust and hope in them. He wore a hair shirt, he ate dry bread and potatoes which were often mouldy; he did penance for those who confessed to him. In little more than ten years after Vianney joined the parish, Ars became a centre of reconciliation, accounting for more than one hundred thousand penitents a year.

He was so tormented in body and soul that he wanted to retire to a monastery in order to relieve the clergy of Lyons of the embarrassment of an ignorant priest; and all he desired there was to do penance for his sins. His sins? God only knows what they were. It is a well-known fact, however, that the nearer a person comes to the light, the more he is aware of his darkness and the more he feels it necessary to receive the Sacrament of Reconciliation to regain the strength to praise the Father with a purified heart.

Deriving benefit from conflict and contrast

Reconciliation has two important aspects: on the one hand, it is a gift; on the other, it is human effort – not towards conformity or the herd instinct, none of these. It is, rather, an effort to benefit from every aspect of existence; and this includes transforming negative experiences into positive ones.

At certain periods in the history of the Church, many priests used the confessional to force the faithful into one mould; they condemned any form of difference or conflict and any criticism of the authorities. But today, even at the theoretical level, the value of diversity has been understood. Especially following the open spirit of Vatican II, dialogue and pluralism are valued; the principle of tolerance taught by Christ through the parable of the 'bad seed which should not be uprooted...', is a virtue that should be cultivated.

Society today accepts conflict as part and parcel of the human condition. So, as such, if it is well handled, it helps to develop and mature individuals and communities. At the psychological level, the individual will find his own identity only when he becomes aware of his 'differentness' – his uniqueness – from all other persons. This discovery is often painful and laborious; hence the expression 'state of conflict'.

At the social level, the claims for justice have gone through a situation of conflict which, unfortunately, has almost always been violent, but they have led society to realise the dignity of the individual. People have been forced to reflect, to proclaim the rights of people to create a more wholesome society.

At the ecclesiastical level, quite a few people have paid dearly for advancing the idea that unity is not uniformity and that the communion of the faithful becomes dynamic through the charity which aims at exploiting the diversity of talents and charisms which will make the Church more and more alive, rich and beautiful in her variety. The state of conflict, if well understood, is great wealth; it makes it possible to discern the gifts of each person and to use the whole of creation intelligently, to get the best out of each situation, wisely managing its apparently contradictory aspects.

Regarding the social dimension of the state of conflict, the

Rite of Reconciliation can be of great value in reuniting the individual to the community. The sacrament doesn't oblige the person to efface his individuality and stop being himself; it offers a chance for him to resume responsibility for his own self and get his relationship with the Father back into focus by using his personal talents to the advantage of the community. Inner conflicts are not made light of; they are taken up and transformed (rebaptised) into something good.

79

And who can sound the depths of the human soul? What a hash of good and evil; what a wealth of loyalty, love, enthusiasm and miserable betrayal! The penitent struggles along his way towards the ideal set forth by God: 'Be holy, because I am holy' (Lv 19:2; Dt 18:3), and highlighted by Christ: 'Be perfect as the Father is perfect' (Mt 5:48). He turns to divine mercy, just as he is, and humbles himself before a priest; he prays that his sin will be forgiven and forgotten and that every little particle of goodness and beauty hidden in the mass of error will be gleaned and made part of the effort of continual renewal which the entire Church has to make. And this is the effort to become ever more new and attractive, to build community each day, to be ever more beautiful in diversity, ever more alive in the family spirit, where conflict is a sign of love, and slights and hurts are immediately forgiven.

Let us rejoice
'Let's have a banquet' (Lk 15:23), declares the father of the prodigal son as he confesses his guilt: 'I have sinned against you'. This confession comes after the rapturous father has run to embrace him and cover him with kisses. The father cuts short this confession: 'Quick, bring the best clothes'. This wonderful parable defies comment.

All cultures and religions attribute great importance to feasting. The community renders homage to the Creator by singing joyful praise at all times, but especially on feast days when some past event which is particularly important for the salvation of all humankind is celebrated.

Usually, a festival centres around a past event which is commemorated and relived. The festival places within the present that very creative spirit and life-giving force which animated that particular moment as an ideal for that particular culture. And it gives us the strength to face the future, holding out, as it does, the hope of better days to come, when our days will be one long feast in the company of all those we have ever loved on this earth.

Preparation for this feast certainly takes a lot of time and effort. Celebration of the feast requires attention to others – an outgoing spirit, accepting others in a joyous dance (even when one is not really in the mood for some people). And, to prevent the feast from losing significance, we need to fuse significant bonds so that, in the future, no one will be excluded from the common rejoicing.

At this point it seems suitable to reflect on Leviticus 16, which is completely dedicated to the rules and prescriptions surrounding the annual celebration of the rites of purification. First, a goat is sent into the desert, symbolically bearing the burden of the sins of the people. Then the community offer sacrifice to God. This rite is still used in many African tribes, both at a community level and at a personal level, as expiation for a particularly serious fault. 'Expiation' here does not mean penance – a self-imposed punishment for a bad action – but, essentially, a purification, rendering us acceptable to the divinity and, so, worthy to join the people in celebration, in singing the praises of the Creator. Expiation takes away sin and consecrates through the shedding of the blood of an animal whose throat is cut in sacrifice.

It is important to note in the Old Testament how God demands, not so much the sacrifice of an animal, as a new spirit, free from sin and considerate of others. The feast of expiation demands that sinners be converted, making a collective confession of guilt. Traces of this can be seen in the Psalms and in the Prophets:

> Let these thank Yahweh for his love,
> for his marvels on behalf of men.
> Let them offer thanksgiving sacrifices
> and proclaim with shouts of joy what he has done.
>
> (Ps 107:21-22)

'Oh, Lord God, great and to be feared, you keep the covenant and have kindness for those who love you and keep your commandments: we have sinned, we have done wrong, we have acted wickedly, we have betrayed your commandments and your ordinances and turned away from them.

'Integrity, Lord, is yours; ours the look of shame we wear today, we, the people of Judah, the citizens of Jerusalem, the whole of Israel, near and far away, in every country to which you have dispersed us because of the treason we have committed against you. To us, Yahweh, the look of shame belongs, to our kings, our princes, our ancestors, because we have sinned against you. Listen, Lord! Lord, forgive! Hear, Lord, and act! For your own sake, my God, do not delay, because they bear your name, this is your city, this is your people' (Dn 9:4-5;7-9;19).

Confession made, and God's forgiveness sure, the people feast, offering the Lord their possessions and trying above all to praise him with a new heart, as, in the words of the prophet, the spirit of the feast lies in acting justly. 'I hate, I scorn your festivals, take no pleasure in your solemn assemblies, when you offer up your sacrifices…. Let justice spring forth like water and uprightness like a never-failing stream!' (Am 5:21-24)

God is mercy and forgiveness. But he is also justice. He will feast and accept songs of praise only when the penitent is reconciled with the community.

In the New Testament the ancient festival of expiation takes on the most sublime significance in the Paschal Feast of Easter. The people need not be sprinkled with the blood of a young bull; the blood of Christ was shed for all on the Cross. The people no longer need to wait for a particular day in order to make it up with God and their fellow human beings. Each time a person wishes to be immersed in the mystery of redemption, he can go – extremely easily and simply – to a priest and involve him in the joy of Resurrection. The festival of reconciliation which is celebrated discreetly in the confessional is echoed by the angels and saints in heaven:

> After that I saw a huge number, impossible to count, of people from every nation, race, tribe and language; they were standing in front of the throne and in front of the Lamb, dressed in white robes and holding palms in their

hands. They shouted aloud, 'Victory to our God, who sits
on the throne, and to the Lamb!', and all the angels who
were standing in a circle round the throne, surrounding the
elders and the four animals, prostrated themselves before
the throne, and touching the ground with their foreheads,
worshipping God with these words, 'Amen! Praise and glory
and wisdom and thanksgiving and honour and power and
strength to our God for ever and ever. Amen. (Apoc 7:9-
12).

'In the same way, I tell you, there is rejoicing among the angels
of God over one repentant sinner' (Lk 15:10).

Your Mercy is Eternal

Give thanks to the Lord for he is good,
for his love is everlasting.
Give thanks to the God of gods,
for his love is everlasting.
Give thanks to the Lord of lords,
his love is everlasting.

He alone performs great marvels,
his love is everlasting.
His wisdom has made the heavens,
his love is everlasting.
He set the earth on the waters,
his love is everlasting.

He led his people through the wilderness,
his love is everlasting.
He struck down mighty kings,
his love is everlasting.
He slaughtered famous kings,
his love is everlasting.

He remembered us when we were down,
his love is everlasting.

And rescued us from our enemies,
his love is everlasting.

He provides for all living creatures,
his love is everlasting.
Give thanks to the God of heaven,
his love is everlasting.

83

(Ps 135)

7

I CONFESS: I BELIEVE AND I PRAISE

In the light of God's Word

Erasmus of Rotterdam was an illegitimate son, orphaned early in life. He found his niche in the monastic life. He was a humanist and contributed to the development of the Renaissance by criticising the social structure of the time and purifying the Church which was at loggerheads with Luther. This purification came about through a difficult and austere life and a constant struggle to reconcile greatness with links in the light of the Word of God. It was a purification brought about also by public confessions, famous among which is the one based on his commentary on the 'Our Father'. Here, I give a free and general summary of the contents: 'Father': We call on God using the familiar name of 'Abba', which means 'Dad' – but do we feel ourselves to be his children? Do we act like sons?

'Our Father': We invoke God as father of us all, but do we feel or act like brothers? Or do we pray rather to our own personal God, without bothering about those around us, or feeling any responsibility for other human beings suffering and dying of want in the remote areas of the world?

'Who art in heaven': Are we tempted to say, 'God, you are in heaven, stay there! Don't bother us with the idea that we should look for you here in this world!' Are we able to discern the face of God in the faces of the poorest of our brothers?

'Hallowed be thy name': Is our life one continuous praise of the Lord, or do we simply use him to push forward our own name – and our own advantage?

'Thy Kingdom come': What steps do we take to bring about God's kingdom here and now, in our midst? Do we do our bit to spread God's kingdom over the whole human family?

'Give us this day our daily bread': Do we do our best to supply the needs of others, to become for them bread for the hungry? Or do we each busy ourselves in obtaining plenty of 'bread' for ourselves and shut out of our consciousness the knowledge that many die each day of sheer hunger. Are we aware of the various kinds of hunger which our brothers suffer, especially the hunger to be loved which can be satisfied by a single look, or a smile, or a gesture?

'Forgive us our trespasses as we forgive those who have trespassed against us': We pray for our own condemnation! How many of us are truly able to forgive?

'Lead us not into temptation': But is it not we ourselves who go in search of temptation – those desirable things which make life more 'interesting'?

'But deliver us from evil': What evil do we want to be freed from? Is it an evil which we love more than the good which we feel to be so unattractive?

Erasmus is not merely speech-making here; he is confessing publicly that he, more than anyone else, is a sinner, who trusts in divine mercy. His example should help us to prepare for confession by examining ourselves in the light of meaningful Bible excerpts.

Among the directives given by Vatican II for the fitting celebration of the Sacrament of Reconciliation we find these words: 'The Sacrament of Penance must begin with a reading from the Word of God, as it is through his Word that God calls us to repentance' (*Rite of Confession* n. 24). The 'Word' shows us how much the Father has done to help us and fosters in us the will to appeal to his merciful love. The 'Word' does not accuse; it reveals his love which calls us. It helps us to focus on our own existence. The Psalms, the Prophets, and many passages from the New Testament help us to analyse our lives closely. If we wish to make a good confession we could prepare for it by meditating on a chapter of the Gospel, begin to understand it, compare it with other passages of the New Testament, and then examine how we are living up to our Christian calling.

Chapter 5 of Matthew's Gospel – the Sermon on the Mount – is a good basis for an examination of conscience. The first eleven verses (the Beatitudes) point out just how far these 'absurdities' have changed our lifestyle; they help us to think in a very different way from people who do not believe in God.

The subsequent verses offer a basis for many confessions: 'Jesus says, "it is written…" – Jesus cites the Law of the Old Testament and adds, "But I say this…"'. This juxtaposition of the Old Testament and the teaching of Jesus helps us to understand our inner polarisation and thus throws light on our journey of faith towards holiness.

When we have examined our conscience in the light of the Gospel, we should then make our confession to a priest who knows us well and is ready to really listen. The confession should start with the reading of the Gospel passage which has shed light on our life.

Confession of faith

The original meaning of the Latin verb *confiteri* is to acknowledge, to admit a fault or crime before a judge. However, from the second century onwards, Christians emphasise two other meanings of the verb: the praise of God found in the Psalms, and the profession of faith.

The sense of 'testifying' to the faith expressed in the Confiteor arose during the time of the persecutions, when Christians were hauled in front of a judge and accused of not recognising the emperor as god. They confessed their 'guilt' – they had not, in fact, offered incense to the emperor's statue or to pagan gods.

As Christians, we need to rediscover the idea that reconciliation is above all an act of faith which fits harmoniously into the Christian life. It is not an isolated act; it is both a point of arrival and a point of departure. The point of arrival is God's mercy, which has led the sinner to take stock of his own life in the light of the love of God the Father, and return to his basic choices.

The point of departure is where, once more, the sinner plunges his being into the life of Christ and gains renewed strength to continue his journey again in God's grace.

Reconciliation through the sacrament becomes a profession of faith by proclaiming the firm belief that God loves us and wants to pardon us and to give us new life. Accusing ourselves of our sin becomes an act of faith, in the same measure as we, like King

David in the 'Miserere', acknowledge the holiness of God in contrast to our own unfaithfulness, and our slow response to his love.

The humble admission of our fault proclaims our faith in divine mercy and in the power of the forgiveness of sins which Christ has given to the Church, in the Word which is the source of our liberation. Just as Yahweh asked Abraham to leave his homeland, just as Christ invited the twelve apostles to leave their work and way of life to follow him, so now the Father invites the sinner to make an act of faith: leave his old sinful ways and start out for that true homeland which God will unfold day by day. To confess is to believe that God's promises will become reality for each individual penitent who is called to newness of life in Christ.

87

Confession of praise

As soon as the Christian becomes aware of God working in his life, he has the spontaneous urge to praise and thank him. Before commencing to confess his sins, he feels he wants to show his gratitude to the Lord for having lifted him out of his miserable situation and led him to that wonderful meeting with the Father.

Moreover, the act of praise and thanksgiving goes beyond the personal level before going into the confessional; it would be very appropriate to include the confessor in giving thanks. The prayer of praise is a rite obliging the pentitent to have a good look at the beautiful things which have happened in his life. Before he accuses himself, it is good practice for him to think back on the positive aspects of life since his last celebration of the sacrament. This way of 'making it up with God' would be helpful, and also useful to the confessor. Often the confessor is relegated to the position of 'taking on himself the burden of sin' or, put more crudely, is used as a kind of spiritual dustbin, rather than an older brother who is sharing in the love of the Father and involved in praising him.

Another reason for beginning confession with praise is to be found in the Old Testament, which tells of the way people approached God when they had sinned. They first recited a detailed list of all the marvels Yahweh had performed for them: covenant, freedom from slavery in Egypt, manna in the desert, water from the rock, the Promised Land.... In this context of

God's merciful love, Israel recognises the grave nature of their sin. Confession then follows. The prayer that Esdra makes while humbling himself (9:6-15) recalls the blessings of God on his people, his patience in waiting for their return to him, the fitting punishments inflicted. But the most beautiful and moving prayer in this vein is the one Moses raises to God, pleading with him to forego the punishment the Chosen People have merited: he presses God to remember the wonders of times past; he urges God to keep in mind that he is faithful to his promises and – supreme impudence – he suggests that God will show up pretty badly if his people of Israel die in the desert.... Conclusion: 'In your most faithful love, please forgive the sin of this people, as you have done from Egypt until now' (Nb 14:19).

In the Psalms, we may find points of reflection in order to justify the opportunity of praising God before confessing our sinfulness. We know that the Old Testament expresses its faith through prayers: *Lex orandi, lex credendi.* When we analyse these prayers, we find that the sinner performs an act of faith while acknowledging the greatness of God's mercy. When he is reconciled with God, he renews his covenant and he is entitled to praise God for his fidelity.

Confession of sin
If it is true that, following the etymology of the word confession, we are not allowed to split the confession of sin from the proclamation of faith and praise, it is also true that confession cannot be restricted to this aspect together with a general admission of having sinned. We already summarised what John Paul II has written about the Sacrament of Reconciliation. The Rite of Penance says: 'The reconciliation with God is required and given through the Minister of the Church' (n. 19). Because sin is a refusal of love and an insult to the Spirit, the Church invites the penitent to celebrate the Sacrament of Reconciliation through a purification, a kind of psychological 'death', while acknowledging his sin. If he wants to be renewed by the grace of the risen Lord, the penitent should live his 'Good Friday', staying three days with Christ in the sepulchre. In this way he will experience reconciliation as a grace which will reunite him with

community life after grafting him on to the vital trunk which is Christ.

In chapter 4, outlining the history of the Sacrament of Reconciliation, we saw how the Church always tried to find the correct way to express the need of people to proclaim their sinfulness, to receive pardon after submitting to a rite which could be meaningful in a given moment of history. The Church is always concerned with giving pardon in such a way that people feel truly liberated from sin. The Church is helped in these times by modern sciences, particularly by psychology and psychoanalysis, and has become much more aware that a person heals himself when he is capable of feeling responsible for his own actions and recognises his own sinfulness. It is of no value to search for excuses. It is psychologically more healthy to recognise simply that you have made mistakes.

Sin, moreover, always has a communitarian dimension: it breaks an equilibrium, deprives people of help, damages others, and prevents grace from reaching other people who could be helped. This dimension should also be integrated in confession: we should feel the need to ask pardon of the community and promise to attend to their needs.

Many people experience that freedom from the burden of their sinfulness; renewed by the absolution, they feel themselves again in God's image and enjoy what was experienced in the beginning of creation when God met the original couple in Eden and strolled with them at sunset in the primordial purity of the cosmos.

Once the penitent asks pardon of a member of the community he feels the strength to look at people without a sense of shame: now he feels at peace with everybody. He is helped by the acknowledgment of his sins to become more merciful towards others. He loves them as they are. He sees them as God sees them and his love for them becomes the measure of which he will be judged at the end of time.

In his encyclical letter *Mystici Corporis* (1943) Pius XII points out that among the various ways of obtaining God's pardon, Christians must continue the tradition of frequent confession. The Pope asserts, moreover, that the confession of our sins increases our self-knowledge; it conserves us in Christian humility; it tends to uproot our evil inclinations; it combats spiritual negligence and lukewarmness; it purifies the conscience; it strengthens the will; it predisposes us to spiritual direction; and, through the effect of the sacrament itself, it increases grace in us. Other reasons for frequent confession could be added: it frees the psyche from a burden which eventually would be unbearable if it mere not removed; it avoids sinking further; it makes permanent conversion easier; it creates in us a new heart; it encourages us to take our place in the Church once more as living and active members.

To express praise

All the Psalms have a common denominator: the need to express praise, to free it from the prison of our human frailties, to give it free rein, to open up a pathway to God. God 'has no need for our praise ... our hymns add nothing to his greatness, but praise obtains for us saving grace. To God belongs praise' (Ps 65:2), but we also discover our own greatness in praising the Creator:

> Praise Yahweh, it is good to sing
> in honour of our God, sweet is his praise.

> (Ps 147:1)

God's praise is beautiful if sung in chorus with others and that's why we should involve the community in expressing the joy of reconciliation. The English proverb which says 'joy is a twin' means that joy isn't fully experienced if it is not shared; joy should be proclaimed from the roof-tops. It is in praise and joyful celebration that we can experience the wisdom of the Bible: 'Joy prolongs life' (Si 30:22).

When the penitent has fully and finally grasped the wonder of Christ's free gift of pardon, he feels the urge to dance and to invite others to move in the same rhythm. He wants to sing aloud his liberation as Moses did when he passed through the Red Sea:

> I shall sing to Yahweh for he has covered himself in glory,
> horse and rider he has thrown into the sea.

Yahweh is my strength, my song,
he is my salvation.
This is my God, I praise him;
the God of my father, I extol him.
Yahweh is a warrior;
Yahweh is his name.

(Ex 15:1-2)

All this should find full expression in the public celebration of the Sacrament of Reconciliation. But even in individual confession – priest and penitent – the hymn of praise should not be left out.

Very probably, those who have committed serious sin don't wait for a public celebration of the Sacrament of Reconciliation; they probably wouldn't go anyway for many reasons. Yet, with the person who has waited long years before asking absolution, the confessor must not only give God's gentle mercy, but allow the penitent to really celebrate God's forgiveness. On various occasions, Bernard Häring told of an experience, which he probably considered a grace that he himself had received, when he was acting as the instrument of God's mercy. He had met a woman who had been a prostitute for many years. When she started to describe her situation, Fr Häring stopped her from going into humiliating details. He invited her, instead, to celebrate God's merciful forgiveness.

So, when other such women turned up at the door of the Redemptorist convent and asked to see Fr Bernard, he asked no questions, knowing who had sent them; he just celebrated with each one. He, himself, was simply grateful to be God's instrument of reconciliation.

The ability to 'unlock the praise within ourselves' depends partly on the sensitivity of the priest but, for the most part, on the penitent's predisposition and preparation. Before confessing his sin, the penitent should first pray a lot to the Holy Spirit to ask for guidance in understanding himself and the joy of meeting the Father. The Spirit will show him that forgiveness is not primarily gained through a detailed description of the sin, but through the acceptance of God's love (cf. Lk 7:47).

So, the penitent could invite the confessor, the minister of God's mercy, to participate in the joyous celebration. Of course, he shouldn't choose a time when the priest will have a great deal of confessions to hear.

Confession can be particularly helpful when the penitent focuses on a particular aspect of his own life. The confession should take the following shape:

92

'I thank God that during this period he has helped me to discover an important aspect of my life. While reading this Bible passage I have understood that....

'But, despite God's goodness to me, I still feel that I haven't done anything about what I have discovered; in fact, my sin is....

'So, because I want to work a bit harder on this aspect, in the future I will engage myself in doing....'

In this way, the two essentials of confession are evident: the penitent has faith in God's mercy which he expresses in praise and thanksgiving for gifts received; he does not hide his sin; he makes a resolution – small and controllable – to make progress in his journey towards truth. If the confessor knows the penitent – better still, if he is his friend – he can easily help him in his search for 'perfection' and rejoice with him in the confession of faith and praise.

One last reflection regarding the 'satisfaction' or the 'penance' to be made after absolution. We have seen how, in the past, the Church administered very severe penances (we would consider them a bit excessive today) before admitting the penitent to the Eucharist. Now, however, in an effort to underline the gratuitousness of God's forgiveness, the Church takes into consideration the humiliation that the penitent willingly undergoes in confessing and has reduced the 'penance' to a symbolic act. I feel that it is not fitting to ask the penitent to recite three Hail Marys as a penance. Praying is not a penance; it is a privilege. Perhaps the formula could be altered, for example: 'In thanksgiving for forgiveness, recite...'.

Alternatively, the confessor could suggest the regular reading of some chapters from the Bible, or the recitation of a Psalm each day in an effort to recapture the grace of the sacrament. It would be even more efficacious to suggest reading some passage from the

Bible with the family to involve them, too, in praise and thanksgiving for forgiveness received. A third possibility would be for confessors and penitent together to find a form of penance most suitable for the spiritual needs. So, if the Sacrament of Reconciliation is celebrated in the community through a penitential rite, especially if the number taking part is small, it would be opportune to conclude it with a common grace, songs and prayers which express the faith of the participants and their praise of God.

Prayer for the Confession of Sins

Blessed be your glorious name
which surpasses all blessing and praise!
You alone are the Lord!
You created the heavens.
You, the Lord God, chose Abram
and made with him an alliance
to give him the land of Canaan.
You worked signs and wonders against Pharaoh,
You divided the Red Sea in the sight of your people,
You guided them in the column of cloud,
You fed them with bread from heaven.
But our fathers acted in great pride
and did not wish to hear your voice.
You are a God who forgives
and you did not abandon them,
even when they moulded a golden calf.
You fed them in the desert for forty years ...
and they ate and were filled and became fat and rebelled!
You gave them over to their torturers.
In their time of trouble they called to you
and in your mercy you freed them many times.
You had patience with them for many long years
in your mercy....

(Ne 9, *passim*)

8

A BANQUET FOR THE REMISSION OF SINS
(MT 22:4)

Come to the wedding feast

'The mystery of the Supper! We nourish ourselves with Christ's Body; we relive his passion; our whole being is filled with grace and guaranteed future glory.' This is the antiphon for the Feast of Corpus Christi; it is packed full of theology and wisdom; the Eucharist is the nourishment of our faith-life; it gives us strength to press on towards perfection; it takes away sin; it gives peace to the spirit and hope in the transformation of the whole cosmos into the glorious Body of Christ.

The man who probed least unworthily into this argument was the French scientist and poet, Teilhard de Chardin. Every little particle of matter spurred his thought and he uttered a sigh of longing for identification with the Body of God's Son. 'Cosmogenesis, Noogenesis (Nous = thought), Christogenesis.' Chardin was expelled from the Jesuit order and grossly misunderstood by the Roman Curia. Yet, only four years after his death, he was recognised by Pope John XXIII and Vatican II.

Once, when Teilhard was alone in a desert region of China, he wished to celebrate Mass, but he had no bread or wine. The sun was going down over the horizon: one huge burning host. He pronounced the words of consecration over his own body, over humanity, over the desert, over the sun: 'This is my body; this is my blood, shed for you and for all men for the forgiveness of sins'. From this solitary invocation came the grain of inspiration and he composed the 'Hymn of the Universe'. 'Receive, O Lord, this whole host which creation offers at the dawn of a new day. This bread – our efforts – I know, are nothing but immense desegregation. This wine – our pain – is also nothing more than a drink which divides. But, beneath this formless mass, you have placed – I am sure of it, I feel it – an irresistible and sanctifying desire which makes us, bad or good as we may be, shout: 'Lord, make us one!....Unflinching, I will place my hand towards the burning bread which you give me. In this bread, where you enclose the germ of every development, I acknowledge the principle and the secret of the future you have in store for me.

'I know; I understand – to take it is to submit myself to powers which will tear me from myself and push me in danger's way, make me labour – the continuous reshaping of ideas, the harsh break with my affections. Hold me in the depths of your heart. Hold me inside you and burn me, purify me, inflame me, let me reach the complete sublimation with the perfect satisfaction of your desires ... to my full annihilation. Oh, Jesus, I abandon myself in life, in death, to your body in its full extension – that is – to the World which has become, through your power and my faith – the magnificent, living crucible where everything melts to be reborn.'

The fire of the Holy Spirit is invoked not only over the bread and wine, but over humanity in its entirety, in order that the whole of humanity becomes Eucharist, thanksgiving. More exactly, the Holy Spirit transforms two fragments of the universe – bread and wine – into the mystery of salvation: Christ becomes food which takes away sin, unifies and renders divine. Herein lies a fascinating and tremendous mystery presented in the form of a banquet to which everyone is invited. The evangelists Matthew (22:1-4) and Luke (14:14-24) tell the parable of the wedding feast which, I think, can equally be applied to the Eucharistic banquet: a king invites his friends to his son's wedding but they turn down the invitation. One says he has to go and inspect the land he has just bought: riches blind us, and so we can't take part in the rejoicing of our one-time friends. Another has bought five teams of oxen: now he has 'power', he is no longer a nobody, so he hasn't got the time. A third has taken a wife (as if a wife were some kind of private property) and is so absorbed in this relationship that he is blind to the needs of others....

When his invitations have been rejected, the king ups and invites everyone else; the important thing is to fill the wedding hall. No one is excluded – good, bad, blind, lame – and all wear the wedding garment which is given to each guest at the wedding-hall door (this is a detail which is not mentioned in the Gospel, as

95

it was a custom known to all). The king comes in to acknowledge the guests and throws out the one guest who has disdained the wedding garment.

It is a privilege to be invited to a wedding; it's a gift. But gifts are not to be received off-handedly; there must be an active response, at least a hand-shake. All the guests must take an active part in the celebration. A gift of something is not so important as the giving of presence at a party.

All this is particularly true of the Eucharistic banquet, where Christ is both host and food for the guests who, for their part, cannot just sit there indifferently, or be distracted, or refuse to eat, when they have accepted the pressing invitation: 'Take, eat … take, drink. Blessed are the guests at the marriage of the Lamb of God'.

'Behold the Lamb of God who takes away the sin of the world'

When John the Baptist points out Christ as 'the Lamb of God who takes away the sin of the world' (Jn 1:29), the Son of God is just about to begin his public life, and is preparing to give his life on the cross for the salvation of humankind. John, the precursor, is alluding to the paschal lamb referred to in Exodus 12: the celebration of Israel's exodus from Egypt (the land of slavery and death – symbol of sin) to the Promised Land, where everyone is invited to a banquet on the Mountain of the Lord. 'The Lamb who takes away….', the use of the present tense is significant. We are in God's time where there is no past, nor future. God is the eternal present.

During the Mass, Christ continues to save us and to take away sin. 'Sin', in the singular, means the range of evil for which humanity is responsible. Christ 'takes away' this evil (the Greek verb can also mean 'taken upon himself, cancelled, lifted, made to disappear). Christ takes on himself the evil of the world, he assumes it in his own flesh, in his own body, to make it die on the cross: evil can be quelled only by sharing it (cf. 2 Co 5:21).

At the Last Supper, Jesus anticipates in the symbol what he will bring about in reality on Good Friday: he gives bread that is broken; he proffers the wine saying: 'This is my blood poured out for the remission of sins' (Mt 26:28).

This very banquet is the seal of the New Covenant announced by Jeremiah: 'See, the days are coming – it is Yahweh who speaks – when I will make a New Covenant with the House of Israel (and the House of Judah) but not a covenant like the one I made with their ancestors on the day I took them by the hand to bring them out of the Land of Egypt. They broke that covenant of mine, so I had to show them who was master. It is Yahweh who speaks. No, this is the covenant I will make with the House of Israel when those days arrive. It is Yahweh who speaks. Deep within them I will plant my law, writing it on their hearts. Then I will be their God and they shall be my people. There will be no further need for neighbour to try to teach neighbour, or brother to say to brother: "Learn to know Yahweh!" No, they will all know me, the least no less than the greatest – it is Yahweh who speaks – since I will forgive their iniquity and never call their sin to mind' (Jr 31:31-34).

And the New Covenant concludes with the forgiveness of sins: the blood washes away guilt, takes away divisions between peoples and is the unifying force among the faithful.

Taken literally, the words of the institution of the Eucharist highlight the meaning that Christ's death cancels sins. The next paragraph takes a look at some writings of the Fathers of the Church where they underline the forgiveness of sins within the Eucharist. However, to understand this point we need to examine it in the light of other Gospel passages, and also in the custom of the Church in its regard.

According to the parable of the invitation to the wedding feast, the person not wearing the wedding garment is thrown out of the banqueting hall and severely punished. Although the parable is mainly concerned with the Final Judgment, it has also been understood as a reference to the Eucharist: if we want to take an active part in the banquet, we must be in harmony with the host and be friendly with all the other guests. The Eucharist can be either a source of life or an occasion of sin: 'He who eats the bread and drinks the chalice of the Lord unworthily will be answerable for the Body and Blood of Christ. Each must therefore examine himself...' (1 Co 11:27-29; 33-34).

The Body of Christ and purification from sins

The early Church recognised in the Eucharist a force for the unification, reconciliation and purification of the faithful. The Greek fathers of the Church are particularly explicit on this matter. St Cyril of Alexandria, the fifth-century Bishop of Alexandria, talked of the healing property of the Eucharist: the Christian takes on the Divine through the actual incarnation of Christ in each receiver of the sacrament: 'Impure silver, when fused with lead is completely purified as the lead takes into itself all the impurities. This is similar to Christ's action in us' (*De adoratione in Spiritu et veritate*, 3). The Body of Christ, entering each one of us, purifies us of all our sins and transforms us into his own Body.

Referring to the miracle which Jesus worked for St Peter's mother-in-law, Cyril calls attention to the touch of the hand of the Son of Man. Jesus could have cured her with a word, but he chose a gesture, a physical contact: 'And we, too, receive Jesus. Come into us! (He comes into us!) If we hold him in our spirit and our heart, he will quench the heat of our wayward wills, give us new spiritual energy and health, so that we will be able to serve him and carry out his holy will' (*Commentarium in Lucam*, IV, 38).

The fourth-century bishop St Gregory of Nyssa used the term 'pharmakon' – medicine stronger than death and source of life (cf. *Discorso Catechetico*, 37:2-3) – in relation to the Eucharist. Theodore of Mopsuestia, a Greek-Syrian ecclesiastical writer of the fifth century and Bishop of Mopsuestia in Syria, commented beautifully and most meaningfully on the prophet Isaiah's vision of the burning coals: 'On the altar there were burning coals, revealing the mystery which was to be transmitted…. Just as the seraph came up to Isaiah and purified the prophet, taking away all his sins with a touch of the burning coals on the prophet's lips, so we must be sure that, receiving Holy Communion, our sins are absolutely "burned up" if we repent with our hearts full of sorrow for our sins' (*Omelie catechetiche*, XVI, 1, 36-38).

Theodore often speaks of the Eucharist as a means of reconciliation and unity among Christians because it cancels out sin which is the obstacle to unity. However, for the Eucharist to have this remedial and unifying effect, the communicant must be wearing the garment of the Holy Spirit received at baptism and regained after sin, through the Sacrament of Penance.

Dionysius of Alexandria (third century) tells this very meaningful story: 'In our area there was a man called Serapion. He was an old man who had always lived a blameless life. But, finally, he succumbed to temptation and sacrificed to false gods, thus becoming an apostate. For a long time he tried in vain to be reconciled with the Christian community, but no one would listen to him. And then he fell ill and was unconscious for three days. On the fourth day, he regained consciousness and called his grandson and said, "Dear boy, how long will you hold this against me? Please, listen to me and absolve me of my guilt. Call me a priest." Having said this, he relapsed into unconsciousness. The boy ran for the priest, but it was night and the priest was unwell; he couldn't leave the house. However, I had given orders that the dying should be absolved if they had asked – especially before falling ill – so that they could die with hope in their hearts.

'The priest gave the boy a particle of the Eucharist, telling him to dip it in water and put it in the old man's mouth. Off the boy went, carrying what the priest had given him. As the boy approached the house, Serapion regained consciousness. "Is it you, my son? The priest couldn't come, but hurry and do what he told you to do and free me from my sin." The boy dipped the Eucharist in water and put it into the old man's mouth. Now, was he not kept alive just so that he could be absolved and his sin forgiven because of the many good actions he had done, and once again be considered a Christian?' (cf. Eusebius, *Storia Ecclesiastica*, VI, 44, 2-6).

This brief reference to the Fathers of the Church can be fittingly concluded with a canon of the Ecumenical Council of Nicaea (325): 'With regard to the dying, the old canon will remain in force; a person on the point of death shall not be deprived of Holy Viaticum, last and necessary. If he does not die after having gained forgiveness through Holy Communion, he will be considered as one who takes part only in prayer. In the same way, the Bishop will use his discretion in granting the Eucharist to any dying Christian who asks to receive it' (c. 13).

Holy things to the holy – 'taste and see …'

When Christ gave the bread and wine to his disciples he said: 'Do this in memory of me'. To 'commemorate' is not simply to call to mind, but to celebrate and ritualise. To 'commemorate' the Last Supper means to repeat it symbolically, to repeat the mystery of redemption brought about on the cross: a body broken and blood shed to take away the sin of the world.

The Church cannot invite all indiscriminately to this banquet. Salvation is for all, the same as the offer to 'taste and see how good the Lord is!' But there is a good reason why the early liturgical rites required the celebrant to hold up the Host and say: 'Holy things for the holy'.* This exhortation, which has now been removed from the rite, was not intended to deter the faithful from receiving Holy Communion; rather, it was meant to encourage in them the proper dispositions of awe and reverence, and to prevent them from going to Communion simply out of habit. We approach the banquet offered for the forgiveness of sins, the sacrament which takes away our daily faults and failings and prevents us from falling into grievous sin.

Moreover, this is the sacrament which does more than forgive sins: it heals the communicant at the very root of his evil; it frees him from his selfishness, and knocks down the ridiculous barriers which we build against each other. Added to this action of purification and the destruction of all evil is the celebration of a mystery: the body of a human being, in contact with the body of the Risen Christ, becomes divine and, day by day, grows into the Absolute, until he is finally consumed in unity with Love himself: 'God, all in all'.

I think that these short illustrations implicitly answer questions such as: Is it necessary to go to confession before receiving the Eucharist? Does the Eucharist eliminate sin without confession to a priest? Is absolution given in the words of the priest: 'May God almighty have mercy on us, forgive us our sins…?'

---

* I was celebrating Mass in the Redemptorist Convent at Gars am Inn, Bavaria, and before the Communion I said, 'Holy things for the holy'. The next day Bernard Häring said, before the Communion: 'Taste and see how good is the Lord'. This was his delicate way of showing me that severity serves no purpose; it is not right to frighten people: The Eucharist is the Sacrament of God's Mercy, the God who hides himself under the poor signs of bread and wine and becomes our food to take away our sins.

The Sacrament of Confession was instituted with the specific aim of taking away sins and for all the other reasons set out in the preceding chapters. However, the Eucharist gets at the very root of sin – our evil inclinations. It bathes us in the grace of the Risen Christ, transforming us into one flesh with him and foregoing bonds of unity among all those who receive the bread of life.

Then again, does the Penitential Rite at the beginning of Mass have the power of the sacrament? Does it really cancel sin, or is it merely a general plea for forgiveness? The answer here is that the remission of sin does not take place at one precise moment of the celebration; it is an ongoing process, a reality in the making, as can clearly be seen in the whole Eucharistic celebration. The penitential dimension runs through the whole Mass from beginning to end. The Confiteor is the first act of penance and there are several further requests for forgiveness. When we recite the Gloria, we say: 'You who take away the sins of the world, have mercy on us'. In the Creed we profess our faith in the forgiveness of sins. After the Offertory the celebrant washes his hands, saying: 'Wash away my iniquities; cleanse me from my sins'.*

In the Canon of the Mass there are several requests for forgiveness. While saying the Our Father, we ask to be pardoned, as we forgive others. Then we repeat three times: 'Lamb of God who takes away the sins of the world, have mercy on us'. By himself the celebrant prays: 'May this communion be not a reason for condemnation, but may it bring health of mind and body'. Finally, each person prays: 'Lord, I am not worthy to receive you, but only say the word and I shall be healed'.

The banquet which reconciles and renders thanks
There is a certain sacramental value in sitting down to eat at the same table together: the meal unites those who break bread together and enjoy the same food and wine (the older the wine, the more important the feast!). The layout of the dinner table has a sacred quality. The way the table is set – the flower arrangements, the foods – all require loving preparation so that

---

* One day my little niece Elisa was serving my Mass. While I was washing my hands she asked, 'Uncle, why are you washing your hands?' I answered, 'Because your uncle is a bit of an ass sometimes, and he does stupid things'. So she replied, 'Wash my hands, too, then!'

the diners can fully enjoy the meal. And no one should be late for the meal, even the daily meal, as human beings need ritual.

What a pity if someone is absent! Perhaps he has refused the invitation to dinner; the empty place then causes the pain of rejection. Perhaps the usual occupant of a place has gone to join the eternal banquet, so a bouquet of flowers could take her place....

If the family has been at loggerheads over some matter, the meal can often be the place for patching up quarrels (angry eaters suffer indigestion!) A simple glance is enough to signal that all is 'forgiven'; all is 'forgotten'.

The father is rapturous at the return of his prodigal son: he has the fatted calf killed. The return, the meeting, the forgiveness and reconciliation all require a feast. God is the happiest of all at this feast; all he desires is to see his children united. And when that happens, God himself sets out the dinner table in heaven. Did he not inspire the prophet with the words:

> Shout for joy, daughters of Jerusalem,
> Israel, shout aloud!
> Rejoice, exult with all your heart,
> Daughters of Jerusalem!
> Yahweh has repealed your sentence;
> he has driven your enemies away.
> Yahweh, the king of Israel, is in your midst;
> You have no more evil to fear.

> When that day comes, word will come to Jerusalem:
> Zion, have no fear,
> do not let your hands fall limp.
> Yahweh your God is in your midst,
> a victorious warrior.
> He will exult with joy over you,
> he will renew you by his love;
> he will dance with shouts of joy for you
> as on a day of festival.

(Zp 3:14-17)

The Son of God, who came to earth to share with us beautiful things which his Father has prepared for us from all eternity, often shared these good things as he sat at table. He began his public life by being a guest at the wedding of Cana. When in Bethany, he dined with Martha and Mary (his friend Lazarus' sisters); he ate to nourish himself, to enjoy the company of his friends and to give them the food which will last for ever (cf. Lk 10:38-42). He ate at table with Matthew, with Zacchaeus the sinner and Simon the Pharisee, and it was at table that he accepted the tears of repentance of the sinful woman (cf. Lk 8:36-50).

His life on earth came to a climax at the Last Supper. He rose from the table and washed his disciples' feet: a sign of the purity required before partaking of the bread and wine of the New Covenant. Communion with Christ's body and blood requires repentance for sin, humility, the ability to wash others' feet and be washed by them (Jn 13:2-20). And all this takes place in an atmosphere of thanksgiving to God, creator of all things for the happiness and good of humankind, and Host at the great banquet, that joy might be everlasting:

> Oh, come to the water all you who are thirsty;
> though you have no money, come!
> Buy corn without money, and eat,
> and, at no cost, wine and milk.
> Why spend money on what is not bread,
> your wages on what fails to satisfy?
> Listen, listen to me, and you will have good things to eat
> and rich food to enjoy.
> Pay attention, come to me;
> listen and your soul will live.

> (Is 55:1-3)

The Eucharistic banquet conserves and ennobles all these human symbolisms – both cosmic and religious: 'Blessed are you, Lord, God of all Creation. From your goodness we have received the bread and wine, fruit of the earth and work of human hands; they will become for us the bread of life and the cup of salvation'.

Each Eucharist summarises the history of the marvels of the Father in the past; renders present Christ himself, the source of life, and pours out the Holy Spirit who purifies from sin, uprooting it altogether; and each Eucharist reconciles the faithful, one to the other, and makes them great in the praise of the Lord – and makes known his great Mercy.

Come!

Come! Let us return to Yahweh.
He has torn us to pieces, but he will heal us;
He has struck us down, but he will bandage our wounds;
after a day or two he will bring us back to life,
on the third day he will raise us
and we shall live in his presence.
Let us set ourselves to know Yahweh;
that he will come is as certain as the dawn,
his judgment will rise like the light,
he will come to us as showers come,
like spring rains watering the earth.

(Ho 6:1-6)

CONCLUSION

'I WILL SING FOREVER OF YOUR LOVE'
(JR 33:11; PSS 90:14; 100:5; 109:1)

'Let he who is without sin throw the first stone' (Jn 8:7). Only Christ can utter words such as these; he throws down the challenge and then bends down and writes signs or words in the sand, which are then cancelled by the wind, just as he, the Son of God, cancels and forgets sin. 'None has condemned you? Then neither will I condemn you. Go and sin no more' (Jn 8:11). No one throws a stone at the adulteress. All of them have sinned in one way or another; the first to leave the place of execution were the oldest.

I began this book by admitting to a difficult period in my life. I could end it with other confessions, because getting older complicates things....

As time passes, we discover that the greatest sin is that of omission: not responding to God's love; being undecided and cynical rather than throwing all our energies into life, forgetting self and becoming pure gift. And the sin consists in a 'situation' where we make the easiest choice, forsaking dreams and fantasies and giving up the fight, perhaps because scratching away has ruined our nails and we are afraid to wear down our fingers too.

Times change and people with them. But do they change for the better? Of course, some things do improve; there is a certain purification in progress. The dignity of each human being is acknowledged now more clearly than before. But, side by side with this, the *sollicitudo rei socialis* shows that the sinful structures of society are gaining strength, and the evil in the world is more and more awesome.

While a sense of hope is redawning in Eastern Europe, in the Amazon silence surrounds the continuing genocide of the Indians, and this is coupled with the barbaric and senseless destruction of their forests. Africa is suffering the disastrous consequences of the colonial era, while élite minorities, corrupt to the hilt, implement policies to the detriment of the poorest. The Middle East is unable to come to terms and find peace.... Times change ... and we go on chanting monotonously that hope lies with the younger generation, yet, for the most part, today's youth seem to be no better than their forebears when they acquire political and economic power.

Qoholeth (c.3) tells us that there is a time for everything but that everything is in vain as the same problems keep turning up in season. Perhaps Qoholeth is excessively pessimistic. As time passes, the face of God, or the conception that humanity has of him, changes. Perhaps, the concept of God as 'Father' – coupled with an awareness of sin – changes throughout the life-span of each human being. When I was a child, I praised God because he is great and Almighty; serving God made me feel important. I needed something bigger, outside of myself; I needed the mystery: in that way I felt secure. Now, in more mature years, I tramp the desert looking for traces of God; I praise him because he, like myself, weeps over the evil of the world.

I am no longer stirred by the 'Absolute', the 'Almighty', because I have discovered the most beautiful aspect of God: his mercy. 'Where evil abounds, grace still more abounds.' Evil, limitation and sin, when seen in the light of God's forgiveness, no longer cause me anxiety. Awareness of my limitations runs alongside the joyous experience that the whole life of Christ is mine to benefit from in the measure in which I see myself a sinner like Zacchaeus, a prostitute as Magdalene was, a deserter like Peter.

Sin, in the context of grace, not only ignites the hope of salvation, but awakens the urge to sing of the mercy of God. This is valid for personal hidden sin and for sin confessed in the Sacrament of Reconciliation: each confessed sin is a spur to pray more and a means of discovering, beyond our limitations and sins, a hidden goodness to be regained.

The Church consecrates priests to make them dispensers of divine mercy and, aware of their own sinfulness, capable of understanding human weakness. They can help sinners precisely because they are 'wounded healers': 'wounded' because they have limitations, 'healers' because they have been set apart above all to administer the Sacraments of Reconciliation and the Eucharist, the feast which they celebrate each day for the forgiveness of sins. All Christians, especially priests, are encouraged to be 'merciful as the Father is merciful'. 'Do not judge and you will not be judged. Do not condemn and you will not be condemned. Forgive and you will be forgiven. Give and you will receive' (Lk 6:36-38). This is the measure of Christian mercy: imitate the Father, be like him; he does not condemn, he forgives, he forgets and gives himself completely. Be like Christ who, several times in John's Gospel, tells us to leave judgment to the Father (cf. Jn 3:17; 8:15; 12:47). Imitate the Holy Spirit revealed to us as purifying fire which consumes sins, not humiliating, but rehabilitating the sinner, and burning away the impurities so that the precious goodness in the soul can shine through.

When a person experiences God's mercy, the forgiveness he receives becomes a desire to be 'gift' for his neighbour. It becomes natural for him to share with the others and to shoulder the other's burden, to put aside the peacefulness of his own life and help another in need. And all this, far from becoming an unbearable burden, becomes a *raison d'être*, a source of that secret joy which comes when a person succeeds in forgetting self and his own sadness, and finds peace in the smile of hope of the poor and marginalised.

Having experienced God's mercy, Paul said: 'When I am weak, then I am strong' (2 Co 12:10). This is the typical response of the person who has discovered that the Lord loves us because of our weakness. Here is the one who decided to take on our miserable dimensions in order to be with us; he it is who matches his stride to ours and becomes 'weak' just because he loves us. Is not love itself a weakness, an ability to measure down, to desire to diminish that the other might grow, a need for an embrace, to act the clown to make children laugh; to be the weak one and do anything just to hear the words: 'I love you'?

A weak person, begging for love, becomes strong when he lives the Beatitudes: 'Blessed be the merciful; he will obtain mercy'. And how do we describe a merciful person? He is courageous; he is trustworthy, because he does things he's not obliged to do; but he acts with his gaze upon the Father, trying to imitate him. The merciful person is he who is not afraid to associate with the sinner (as the Pharisee was) (cf. Mt 9:13; 12:7); he is the person who puts himself on a level with others, is tolerant, helps those in need; the person who forgives others, remembering that he himself has been forgiven through the sheer mercy of God (Tt 3:5).

The merciful person will obtain mercy; this is the Old Testament virtue which was synonymous with justice (cf. Ho 12:17; Mi 6:8), 'rectitude' and 'holiness' (Ps 36:11; 40:11), 'peace' (Jr 16:5). This virtue is like joy: it cannot be savoured alone; it needs to be shared with a community as a feast of mercy. The sinner who raises his eyes to heaven is a signal for feasting among the saints and the delight of the Father; 'Come to the feast!'

God invites us to allow ourselves to be reconciled, because it is good for us: reconciliation frees us from silly anxieties, gives direction to our lives, knocks down the barriers which stop us from loving and being loved, puts us back in harmony with creation, which itself is humiliated and wounded by our selfish choices.

Responding to the invitation to reconcile himself, the sinner confesses his sins. It is an act which requires a humiliation, an owning to a fault committed, but it is, at the same time, a mark of his greatness as it 'gives rein to praise, that praise which was bound in sin'. In this sad world where error spawns anguish, the Sacrament of Reconciliation takes on a prophetic value: it proclaims the sundering of the bonds of evil which bar us from our own greatness in proclaiming the mercy of God.

Once he has been absolved, the sinner is welcomed by the community rejoicing in the risen Lord around the table where bread and wine are offered 'for the forgiveness of sins': the body and the blood of Christ re-establishes with the Father the Covenant of Love, and roots out the basis of all evil: selfishness. The sinner is healed and sings joyfully once again: 'I will sing of God's mercy at all times'.